Prais

'A gripping and brilliantly w   s
survival, up there with the very best of adventure memoirs such
as *The Salt Path* by Raynor Winn or Cheryl Strayed's *Wild*.
Kathryn Heyman has pulled off an amazing feat, giving a true
story of trauma and recovery all the narrative pull and beauty
of the best of novels. Her account is a literary work that will
stand the test of time and has international bestseller written all
over it.'   —Louise Doughty

'*Fury* took my breath away. Heyman writes with such brio,
muscularity and physicality; her trademark humour, honesty
and energy vibrate on every page. This memoir is a triumph,
the journey it tells of a girl shaping herself in her own fashion
a salutary reminder of the crushing oppression that girls face
every day and the courage – and the fury – that it takes to get
out from under that.'   —Jill Dawson

'Heyman has every kind of courage there is. As a girl she dares
the world to treat her as equal. It doesn't, but she holds on to her
ambition and her imagination in the face of the thousand shocks
that female flesh is heir to; the litany of sexual terror women
and girls dodge each day. And so, *Fury* is searing, thrilling and
redemptive.'   —Anna Funder

'This powerful, ultimately joyous memoir shows how—in the
teeth of a gale – a damaged girl can find her own strength, and
fight for her own path.'   —Jennifer Byrne

'A vital addition to the national conversation. A searing,
moving, deeply honest achievement.'   —Nikki Gemmell

'Distressing, thrilling, immaculate – and vitally important.'
                                                      —Clare Wright

'*Fury* is that old, old story in which a vulnerable girl becomes a victim, but it is made new by Kathryn Heyman's bold, brave and poetic voice. She tears open what it means to exist in a predatory male world. It's a confronting and compelling memoir, and also an uplifting one: the great triumph is in the art, the storytelling, the very words, that have saved her.'
—Debra Adelaide

'I can't remember when a book gripped me so tight and so hard. This stunning, harrowing memoir is a fierce testament to the power of words and books to save a life ... an intoxicatingly triumphant story that defies the odds, as a fearless young woman's spirit refuses to be crushed by the law or defeated by a roiling sea.'
—Caroline Baum

'Each chapter is like a punch in the guts. It will move you, shock you and—yes—make you furious.'
—Jane Caro

'Moving and ultimately triumphant, a story of survival and reinvention about a woman who refuses to let the system, her family and the men from her past, destroy her will to live and the truth of who she really is. Inspiring and brave.'
—Sarah Lambert

'This sensitive, searching book broke my heart. Heyman transcends her harrowing Australian girlhood by taking herself to sea. That she regains her body and her self is a triumph. Utterly compelling.'
—Carrie Tiffany

'Heyman is a woman looking at the past with clarity and speaking to the present clearly: *enough ...*'
—Bri Lee

FURY

KATHRYN HEYMAN

myriad

First published in the UK in 2021 by
Myriad Editions
www.myriadeditions.com

Myriad Editions
An imprint of New Internationalist Publications
The Old Music Hall, 106–108 Cowley Rd, Oxford OX4 1JE

First printing
1 3 5 7 9 10 8 6 4 2

A CIP catalogue record for this book
is available from the British Library

ISBN (pbk): 978-1-912408-64-1
ISBN (ebk): 978-1-912408-65-8

Designed and typeset in Palatino
by WatchWord Editorial Services, London

Printed and bound in Great Britain
by Clays Ltd, Elcograf S.p.A.

For Stephi Leach,
who saw the woman that the girl might become,
and helped me to see her too

BLOODY BONAPARTE. He shouted into the air, the words flapping away from him like seabirds. *You fucker. This fucking gulf.* His shouting turned to howling, the pitch running higher and higher. His face lifted to the storm-whipped sky, a fist raised to the wheeling seabirds, their clacking squeals drowning him out. I caught only occasional words: *fucker, Bonaparte, useless*. Some words flew out to me, teetering on the metal trawling boom, the rust sliding into my palms, the storm spray spitting up. The deck seemed an ocean away, never still. Even with the rolling of the boom, I could feel the constant tremor in my legs. I was fifty metres from the safety of the deck, standing on a piece of metal less than a foot wide. Twenty metres below me the dark ocean rose and fell, surging with its foamy mouth.

Rust, the taste of it, mixed with salt, with fear. Forever after this, I will associate the smell of rust with fear, with the arse-clenching terror of almost-certain death. Despite all the moments that led me to that trawling boom, and that storm in the middle of the Timor Sea – all the moments of near-death, near annihilation – this is the one that turns my stomach to liquid years, decades, later. Even now, writing this on solid ground, my legs have begun to tremble. My body, asking me not to remember. We have got this far, my body and me, without trawling up the mud and mess of it all, the memories that made me.

1

On the deck, next to the gob-spitting, fuck-shouting skipper, the deckhand – Davey – held a light above his head. Each time another wave roared up, the light was swallowed by the water and the dark. Behind each loss of light, he called, *Sorry, I'm sorry.* Sorry not just for the loss of light but for his wounded arm, bandaged to the shoulder, which meant that it was me out there on the slippery boom, trying to pass tools down to Karl, the first mate suspended from the broken boards with a spanner clenched between his teeth while the waves roared.

We should have hauled the nets up when the storm started. We should have learned some skills, had a less desperate, more capable crew. We should have – *he* should have – listened to Karl. We should have battened down, settled down, gone to ground. All the should haves, useless when the thick salt spray is in your face, when the black night is whipped by wind and wild rain. Desperation made us keep going, lowering the nets when we could hear the rumble across the sea, could feel the lift of the wind, the waves whitening as the sky turned dark. Karl had looked up at the sky, sniffed the air, and called up to Mick in the wheelhouse, 'We shouldn't shoot away. It's going to turn bad.' Mick had clambered out, standing with legs wide on the tray, hands on his hips, eyes narrowed while he followed Karl's gaze. His first skipper's job, a favour from the uncle who owned the fleet. It made him anxious, unsure of his own footing. The nets dangled above us; Karl's hand hovered on the winch. Karl waited, and then added, 'It looks like it'll be rough, skipper. What do you reckon?' He might as well have been an alpha dog, a wolf, rolling over to show his belly. But it didn't work. When Mick shook his head and said, 'We can't afford to miss a catch,' Karl nodded and said okay. It was only after the skipper scrambled back to the wheelhouse that Karl said, 'He doesn't know anything about what it's like out here.

2

He couldn't read the gulf if it was printed on a poster in front of his stupid face.'

The booms on the *Ocean Thief* stretched out on either side of the boat, wide arms forming a crucifix across the moving palette of the sea. On a good day, these trawling booms glinted with tropical heat. Inhabited by temporary colonies of seabirds – terns with punk hairstyles, gulls spreading their white wings, sometimes a sea hawk – on those days they had something soothing, domestic, about them. A marine Hills hoist, an aquatic, static windmill. But not that day. Not that night.

My bare feet curved, my toes gripping the narrow width of the bar holding me unsteadily as the boat lurched. Following Karl's instructions, I'd hooked my arms over the narrow band that formed a sort of rail above the boom. Mouth dry, terror at the back of my throat, I leaned forward, clutching a Dolphin torch in one hand, the beam rising and falling as the wooden boards below me slapped up and down with the slide of the ocean. Waves smacked against the boards with the force of a punch. The metal cut into the softness of my armpits. Framed by the black of the water snapping at his feet, Karl's face flashed in and out of the light, his hand reaching up to mine.

The belt of tools at my waist dug into me, the handle of something – a spanner? a wrench? – stabbing into the flesh at my hip, a relief from the pressure of the thin rail across my belly. Karl shouted up at me, but the storm whipped his words away. *Ack. Asser. Ick. Uck.* It was all noise, a wash and a roar of noise: Karl's snippets, half-words that disappeared into the storm; the punch-roar of the waves; Davey on deck calling *sorrysorrysorry*; the skipper behind him fist-shaking, shouting; the shriek of dolphins trailing the fishing boat; my own bloody heart, the thudding of it.

We had heard the first crack of thunder earlier, but we put the nets out anyway. We'd held to the deck as the six-berth fishing trawler slid up and down relentless waves, and, when the rain started pummelling us, huddled in the galley. It was the shrieking of the dolphins that called us back out on deck, pods of them trailing the boat, the strange squeal louder than the storm. Karl and I leaned out on the gunwale then, squinting into the rain until we could see. The boards that held the nets steady had broken. We couldn't get the nets up without mending the boards. And if we couldn't pull up, with unstable nets heaving in a thrashing sea, we were unbalanced, likely to be forced over, or under, to become one more weekend news story of boats lost in the Gulf.

Karl raised his face again as another wave hit. *The screw. Iver. Need. Mash.*

Folding myself in two, I leaned further down, a screwdriver dangling from my hand. Karl reached up, but not close enough. My foot lifted off the boom, while my arms gripped tighter. On the deck behind me, Davey shouted a warning. The boom lifted then fell and the boards smashed towards me. The torch dropped from my hand just as another wall of water surged, pounding into my face, my eyes, until I was blinded, only feeling the turn of metal beneath me. I grabbed at something near, while the wall of the world – dark, impenetrable – came closer. Terns screeched, counterpointing the shrieking of the dolphins and the rattling inside my skull, a bass reverberation. Karl's voice sounded below me, a call, a warning, and then there was the clang of the chains and a sudden smack to my face. The thickness of blood then, and soundless dense black.

THE PARTY WAS in Sydney, in an apartment full of people I didn't know. Drama students, mainly. Beautiful people, funny people, smart people. A friend, Penny, had dragged me along for reasons that I still can't fathom. I do remember what I was wearing. I'll always remember that, I suppose. Earlier that year I'd found, in a charity shop, a green-and-black-checked vinyl trench coat with a pointed collar and a neat belt. Inside the vinyl I sweated like the inside of a car, but it was worth it. I had a little skirt on underneath, and green pointed boots. Boiling, sweating, and the fattest girl in the room, I kept drinking. And I kept drinking, waiting for someone to notice me, to speak to me, to find me funny, or interesting, or to like my careful green trench, to notice how witty it was, how ironic. But none of these things happened.

Penny stayed in the kitchen, running her hand down the arm of someone called Jeff, who'd just landed a role in a new film about the heroes of the Kokoda Track. He had one line, and he kept repeating it in the kitchen, while Penny tilted her head back and laughed, revealing the long line of her throat. His Adam's apple bobbed when he watched her laughing, the dusting of pale brown hair moving like wheat stalks.

That head tilt, that laugh, that hand slipping easily down a muscled arm: I couldn't do it, couldn't quite understand it. When I tried, the laugh came out broken, the hand too firm on the arm, the head thrown back so fiercely that I could hear my own neck crick. It was a girl thing. I'd watched it right through

5

high school but even now, at twenty, I still couldn't understand it. It looked like a performance, all of it – the hair flicking, the gathering in giggling groups, the coded language. But I'd somehow missed the rehearsal notes.

In high school, I once watched Sylvie Fagan standing in a group of boys, listening, laughing, smoothing her legs together. As she listened, she rubbed one newly shaven calf against the other. She looked like an elegant flamingo. When I tried it the next day, I lost my balance and tottered sideways, cheeks flaming red, my audience of boys doubling over with laughter. Also, I talked too much, tried to match the boys with their jokes and stupidity, tried to outdo them.

In that apartment, with Penny in the kitchen and me in the living room, I balanced on the arm of a sofa, kicking my green boots out in front of me. Three girls danced in front of a faux fireplace while an American man shouted encouragement. They followed each other seamlessly: hand up, hip jut, click and turn. Hips swaying, shoulders shimmying. Those girls. Their hips were narrow in a way mine never could be, their hair long and shining. They seemed like girls from hair product advertisements. I kicked the pointed toes of my boots and pretended not to notice, not to care. The dancing was smooth, the shimmying mesmerising. But if I watched, if I gazed at the dancing trio, I would be – what? Not a girl? A man? I couldn't understand what I was. If I didn't want to dance like the dancing girls, shimmying for the shouting, cheering American, what sort of girl was I?

I'd brought cheap wine, shared with Penny. She'd brought me. As an audience? As the plainer friend? She was a girl who'd got the rehearsal notes. On her bedroom wall was a framed collage of high school photographs: her long hair sliding down her back while she leaned against a boyfriend with his wetsuit peeled to his waist; another of her with a team of girls, their pretty heads close together, eager faces, long legs.

The wine went quickly. I perched on the sofa, smiling mysteriously with my lips closed over my crooked teeth. I'd read, in *Rolling Stone*, a description of a famous woman, the muse to a musician and then to a designer, who could stand alone in a crowd looking completely calm, completely contained. Sometimes I stood in front of my mirror, experimenting with looking contained, mysterious. Smiling into the distance, deep in thought. But not so deep that I couldn't be approached. If I was lucky – mysterious enough but approachable enough – I might get to be a muse. The midwife to someone else's creativity.

Some time after midnight, I emptied the second bottle and trip-trapped to the kitchen on my new green boots. They clacked on the tiles like teeth. Penny was tangled in the Kokoda Track man, her mouth swallowed, her hands on his neck. I stood in the doorway and waited.

In primary school, girls had best friends and named them, declared them like crushes, signing up to a public kind of coupledom. *She's my best friend. Why are you talking to my best friend?* And Lisa O'Daniel was my best friend. She was, consensus had it, the prettiest girl in school. And I was the girl whom pretty girls would choose to be their second-in-command. The not-too-pretty girl, the more-or-less-plain girl who could scrub up all right. In our last year of primary school her family took me with them on a camping trip. I was the poor friend, always the poor friend, dragged along to entertain Lisa, and I knew that this was my job. But this time, there was a boy. Jack? Jake? I can remember his long arms, the way his hair bushed on top of his head, his large teeth. I can remember the way he took my hand on a walk down the bush track to the beach and I looked back, worried that Lisa would see. When he left the campsite, packing up his car with his parents for the rest of their once-in-a-lifetime road trip, he kissed me chastely on the cheek while Lisa watched, and for the rest of the camping trip I was alone. But before he left, with his parents waiting in their hire car, he ran back and whispered to me, 'She thinks she's better than you, but it's the other way around. You're better, way better,' and then he kissed me on the mouth, his lips leaving a warm imprint. I'm still not sure who decided that there was a competition: the boy, or Lisa, or me.

In high school, Lisa called me over to her house one night. A crowd had gathered in her front garden, forming a circle with Lisa O'Daniel at the centre: they whooped and cheered while Lisa called me a liar, a backstabber, a slut.

And I told Lisa O'Daniel that I had never been a backstabber.

In the Sydney kitchen with the Kokoda Track man, there was no chanting circle. There was just Penny and the bobbing Adam's apple of the newly minted film actor. After a while, Penny turned her head to me, eyebrows raised, and said, 'What?'

I said, 'I think I'm ready to go.'

'Then go.' Perhaps her eyes rolled when she turned back to the actor. Or a shoulder shrug, shaking me off.

I opened my mouth to say, I don't know where I am, or how to get home, and then I closed it again. I felt for the folded notes in my pocket.

The party was on the outskirts of town. The party was full of strangers.

But the stranger who was dangerous was not in that room.

OUTSIDE, THE AIR vibrates with the wetness of spring. Lights blur in and out of focus: cars, streetlights? I can't tell; can barely tell which is sky and which is road. Both are black, shining with the reflection of a plump moon. Leaving the party, I raised my hand, muttered a drunken goodbye to the room. No one noticed me go, no one raised a hand or an eyebrow as I stumbled out onto the street, my hand luffing in the air, a flag without country, without purpose.

Pieces of gravel flick up beneath my scrabbling feet, somehow falling into my boots, inching down beneath my soles. Bending over, I try to slip my hand into the top of the boot, wriggling my fingers about to find the bits of pebble worrying at my toes. When I stumble, tumbling face first towards the road, there is no one to laugh with, but I laugh anyway, as though I am surrounded by friends hooting joyously at my drunkenness. Nonetheless, I'm sober enough to think this: I need a taxi. It will no doubt use the last of my week's wages, the small amounts I eke out daily. But still.

It's hard for me to inhabit my own skin, now, looking back at this staggering, arm-waving girl. Sometimes, now, I see them on the street, girls like me, barely able to stand, and I want to, it's true, wrap a cardigan around their shoulders, take them home to sleep it off, to sober up. Mother them as I was not mothered, that's what I want to do. I cannot look at these girls without a

9

rush of fear. I can barely look back at myself, at my shiny coat, my green boots, my bare thighs pimpling in the cool air, my ridiculous faith that the world would take care of me.

Everything is soft: the air, the night, the ground, my legs, my tongue. My hand loose, the arm beneath it unsteady, the ground beneath my feet billowing gently. If the story had been different, if the ending to the evening were different, I would remember this night – if I remembered it at all – as one of many warm spring nights, blending in casual reminiscence. Jasmine scenting the darkness, balmy air on the arms, the pleasures of youth. That's what I would recall, if I had any recollection at all. If I were not required to remember.

Later, when they ask me what I recall, I will try to tell them. I will try to make it seem that I do remember, because that is what they tell me to do. The Crown prosecutor, who is allegedly on my side, tells me this just before he tells me for the third time that I am not on trial. I meet him only once before the court case: his vowels are round, his chin long. I am distracted by the point at the end of his nose, like a mole drawn on a cartoon witch, and by the fat clamminess of his voice, as though his words are swallowed before they are spoken. He keeps his eyes on the windowsill behind me, or on the papers on his desk. He says, 'What do you recollect? Try.'

Then, glancing down at my too-tight top, he adds, 'Is there anything you need to tell me? Is this what you were wearing?'

I wore French knickers, the kind with loose legs. I loved them, the way they slid and slipped against my skin, the cut of them wide and free like 1930s tennis shorts. Penny, the friend who took me to the party, gave them to me as a birthday gift. She'd wrapped them in thin tissue paper and wrote a note on a piece of card: *Something beautiful for a beautiful year.* Silky, soft; they were a lustrous pearl colour, the shine of them reflecting the light. I suppose they reflected the streetlights outside as the taxi swerved across the white lines. Perhaps the light of his wedding ring was reflected too.

But anyway, when the clammy prosecutor asks me what I remember, the truth is that I recall only this: the slapping of the air, the whirring of the lights, the rushing of the ground. Everything is thick and slow, my movements dulled by the cheap wine. I remember that it felt pleasant being outside, away from the beautiful people, away from Penny and her need for an audience. Perhaps I shouted or whooped into the empty street, arms spread wide, inviting the world to come and get a piece of me if it thought itself hard enough. Did I have a 'you'll be sorry' song stomping through my brain? It's possible. Anything is possible. My clawing at the soft air, the taxi lights coming closer, the safe and familiar white of the taxi swerving towards the kerb. Like a painting, or a cinema poster, this part of that night carries a semi-lit haze over it. And his face, leaning across, peering through the window, smiling. A smooth face, warm, bearded. I do remember his face. I don't make that up. Sweat sheening on his forehead.

I'm in the front seat of the taxi. This is Australia. We are egalitarian here. Years after this, when I live in Oxford and jump in and out of black cabs, I will feel myself unfurl with gratitude for the windows dividing passengers from drivers in taxis, the back seat so clearly separated.

My vinyl coat, so sixties, so retro-chic, sticks against my skin in the warmth of the taxi. My arms are wet in the sleeves. Perhaps I ask him to turn the air-conditioning down. My memories now, like the memories of very early childhood, are without words, are purely bodily memories, a series of sensations in the dim dark. Heat. Light. Swerve. Sick. The formation of a single word: *no*.

I must wriggle out of the coat, sliding against the stickiness of it, or at least drunkenly get half an arm out. When I am picked up later, I have one arm in and one arm out, holding my hands up in the middle of the road while the headlights of another car bear down.

It's that second taxi driver who I remember, his arm beneath mine, his grey hair curled around his ears. Running, shouting. Somehow, I remember – or imagine – that he wears striped pants, too baggy for his skinny frame. Orange flashes across the road, his hazard lights blinking on, off, where he stopped short in the middle of the lane, running from the car to the girl – me – stumbling, tumbling, in the centre of the road. His hands under my arms as I buckle. A towel retrieved from the boot of the car and wrapped around my bleeding leg; his cardigan draped over my shoulders.

'I have a daughter your age,' he says. 'If anyone ever – if they tried to—' He stops, looks away.

I wonder what it must be like to have a father who cannot speak for love of you.

By then, the cold air, the resistance of the tarmac underfoot, the crunch of gravel, the shock of my own scream – I think that these things have sharpened me, woken me from the dull daze.

But perhaps they have not.

Because I also remember this: the grainy brown counter of the police station, my hands spread out, while I say, 'I've been—'

I stop then, try to gather myself. Pat at my hair, attempt to wipe at the make-up that I know will be smeared panda-like beneath my eyes. 'I think I've been raped.'

The sergeant in charge is not young. Tall and frowning, he makes me think of my father, himself a policeman. Disappointed, held upright by a thread which could be anger, and with a long, horse-like face. Full of bluff and blunder.

His eyebrows are grey, scraggling across his forehead as he raises them. Holding his hands up, trying to slow me down. 'Whoa. Let's start at the beginning.'

I repeat my words, trying for more certainty, trying for the beginning. 'I've been raped.' The words feel wrong in my mouth, as though the active person in the sentence is me, being raped, rather than the man doing the raping.

The tall constable leans across the counter, looking me over as though I'm a second-hand car. He says, 'I don't know about that, girly, but you've certainly been drinking.'

This man, I think, is wasted on the front desk. With his investigative skills, he should have been a detective. I've lost count of what I drank at the party with the beautiful people who were mystified by my presence. I've long ago lost count of the number of times I'd been called *girl*, or *girly*. But, because on some level I understand that I am being assessed here, in this vomit-coloured police station, I am careful with my words.

'Yes,' I say, 'I have.' I try to make it sound apologetic, and then I add, 'But I've also been raped.' I correct myself again: 'I think I've been raped.'

'You think,' he says, his lip stretching back across his teeth, like my father's mare when he bridled her, her head tossing, her eyes turning white. 'It's the kind of thing you might be certain of.'

In the dark of the taxi, the alcohol swarms through my blood, my head tipped back against the vinyl of the car seat. Warmth floods over me and my tongue becomes heavy, my head begins to nod. I assume – but I can't be certain – that I give the driver the address before I drunkenly flop. I think I do. I think I wave my hand and slur the suburb. I can still speak, although the syllables run together and the making of complete sentences is a little beyond me. Perhaps I giggle, although my drunkenness at this stage is rapidly descending from the raucous to the morose variety. Laughing for my imaginary audience as I toppled forward on the gravel while trying to dig out pebbles from my boot – this seems long ago, days ago. Pipe music plays on the radio, the kind of song that might call you to prayer, and, with the heat, I am lulled into a dozydrunken sprawl. My head lolls, my arms flop, my knees drop. I'm vaguely aware of him turning the music up, his hand on the radio dial. Vaguely aware, too, of the way his hand brushes against my leg as he moves it back to the wheel. But then the road is stretching ahead, and the lights outside are flickering, and the taxi takes a turn and another, and then my mouth drops open, and my head bounces lightly against the window; I am dimly, ever so dimly, aware of a little dribble limping down my chin. Pipes drift through the night, which seems to be getting longer. Vanilla, cloying, over-sweet, clotting the air.

I am drifting, dropping into the depths. Like a dream, when you're aware of being in a dream, but also wanting to be awake. Those dreams when you can hear people talking, when you try to open your mouth and say, *I'm here, I'm right here, I can hear you, I'm not asleep at all*. The terror of those dreams, of trying to claw up to consciousness. This is where I am, down in the deep, with something troubling me, calling me up to consciousness. My legs sprawling, there is the sensation of another brush across my thighs. I close my eyes tighter, turn slightly in the seat. A hand now, squeezing my leg. Sloppily, I slap at the air.

Alcohol has numbed my tongue, made it heavy in my mouth, so that the words *stop that* come out as *stoooiii*. But it does not matter because he does not hear me or my words; he does not feel my hand batting at the air. Or, more precisely, he does not care to hear that or to feel this. Now, when I try to bring this to mind, it's still the swirl of the street that comes back to me, the way the taxi veers off course, looping across the road, as the driver slips his finger into the shiny silkiness of my new knickers. Now I assume it is his own excitement that makes him swerve, his panting sheening face unable to concentrate equally well on the road.

It is the swerving that brings me more to myself, with a dip of my stomach matching the lurch and then the sudden stop of the car, the wheels skidding slightly, a scraping on gravel, a bounce as the wheels hit dirt or grass. Deep down, in my deepdowndozydrunken self, the lurching echoes. I can still feel the twist of nausea now, all these years later, writing this; the bubble of saliva prickling at my mouth. There is a tear, a tug, the resistance of the buttons on the knickers. A small pop as one button gives way, rolling to the floor.

And then, a heavier lurch, the stab of pain inside me, my vaginal canal forced open, the breath of the taxi driver on my face, his beard on my nose, his voice, his breath, and the thrust of in-out-in-out. My body is limp, my limbs not entirely obedient, but I flail at him. Arms and legs, both, begin to obey the slow and slurred commands from my brain, and though there is little strength in me, my sudden buckling, my fists tearing at his hair, startles him. Enough, anyway, that I am able to shove against the door and tumble out, backwards, like a worm, landing buckled on gravel, tearing the skin from my shins and from my hands. Stones lodge in my knees as I scrabble, hauling myself up to all fours, stumbling to my feet. I run, then, pitching towards the road, towards the gleam of headlights growing closer, making holes in the darkness.

I JUMPED FROM A CAR at fifteen. Ran through a field, grass burrs catching on my clothes, pampas grass cutting me when I scrambled over the back fence to a stranger's garden.

Sylvie Fagan introduced me to hitchhiking. We were fourteen. It was one of those sweltering Australian Sundays when steam rises off the tarmac. Heat blanketed us in the fibro rented house I lived in. She'd stayed overnight – a rare sleepover for me. Rare for me to have friends over, to overcome my mother's embarrassment about our house, an embarrassment I had absorbed. I'd learned to apologise for the smallness of the house, for the tiny kitchen, the uncarpeted floors.

We'd lived in the police house in Boolaroo – place of many flies – while my father blustered and blistered and bellowed until my mother found a way to leave, and then we moved to the first of many tiny rentals. Most of the sisters had gone by then, licking their own wounds, and when the last sister left I was allowed to move into my own bedroom. Until then, I'd shared a double bed with my mother. At night, her loneliness swelled up, suffocating me, so that I would lie awake, trying to breathe, trying to resist being swallowed by the force of her need. I was nine years old when the last sister left; nine when I got my own room, my own bed. Nine when the curtain of loneliness and sadness stopped squeezing my chest each night. It was still there, though, years later, pulsing through the house like breath.

And then, fourteen, and hitchhiking with Sylvie Fagan to Redhead Beach. We'd set out with bus money in our purses, our string bikinis peeping out beneath little cotton dresses, but while we were waiting at the bus stop two boys in a white Valiant skidded to a stop in front of us. The boy in the passenger seat had long grainy blond hair, a tiny smattering of pink pimples running down the side of his cheeks. He said, 'Are you girls hitching?' And as I shook my head, my lips together, mute, Sylvie nodded, opened the back door, and said, 'Redhead Beach. Thanks, boys.' She seemed like a twenty-year-old, like someone in a movie. With her flamingo legs, her flicking hair, she'd learned the lessons of how a girl was to be in the world. Open, beaming, up for it.

Being a girl, Sylvie told me, that was everything. We had it all, she told me. We ran the world. She was Beyoncé before Destiny's Child. And she loved it, being a girl. I watched her, curious, furious. There she is, painted in my memory: hip jutted, eyebrows raised, her long hair flying back.

Vinyl stuck to my thighs, there on the back seat of the car taking the side roads to Redhead Beach. Wind puffed at my face through the open window, and I stared out at the road, saying nothing while Sylvie sat forward on the seat and babbled to the boys cheerfully. When they dropped us at the beach – right outside the surf club – the boy in the passenger seat said, 'See you later, quiet mouse,' and grinned at me so that his mouth made a lopsided curve and my stomach flipped pleasingly. Three hours later, when we were ready to go home, we didn't bother walking to the bus stop, we just stood on the main road with our thumbs pointing out and our dresses tucked up so that you could see the curve of our thighs.

And so, at fifteen, I stand on the road in the dark, my thumb outstretched, an eager smile plastered on my face. I am going to Lisa O'Daniel's place. There are no buses to her house. My mother is working night shift, and so I hitchhike because otherwise I would be stuck in the tiny house with my new stepfather, his neatly ironed jeans belted beneath his tiny bantam chest, a stream of rage ready to burst out at the slightest provocation.

It's not yet summer, and the dark sets in early. I stand under a streetlight so that I will be seen. Smiling, trying to look pretty-but-tough. Gravel crunches, small pebbles scattering up and nicking my shins when the station wagon stops in front of me. Beneath the yellow gloom of the streetlight, the shadow of the wagon stretches to the end of the road, my own shadow blending into it.

Beneath my hand, the chrome of the door handle is icy; I slip my jumper down over my palm. Inside the car, a thin light glows with the open door, a vague grey light like the inside of a fridge.

'Are you going to the bay?'

My hand is still on the door, ready to run if I need to, ready to jump in if the answer is yes.

The driver twists in his seat, looking back at me. He says, 'It's very dangerous to hitchhike.'

I want to use his real name, the boy at the wheel of that car. I want to name him, as well as show him. I want him to somehow find his way to this book, to remember the boy he was, and what he did, what he tried to do. His name is Tony de Ropp.

His name is Mark St Clare.

His name is John Witt.

His name is any of the names of the boys you have known. The nice boys, polite boys, who hold the door open. Boys who become men wearing suits or jeans or shorts, nodding in the meeting room and trying to keep their eyes above your neckline. Men who forget, who try to forget, the boys that they were.

He is tall, his face moon-shaped like John Denver's and, like John Denver's, his hair is the colour of straw, with a square fringe feathering above his eyebrows. He knows my sister. He went to school with my brother. He has been to our house. He knows my name.

I thought, when I began writing this book, that it was just the story of how the ocean saved me so unexpectedly. A story of how I was made new. But then I have to ask this: why does a girl get on a boat with four men, strangers all, and head out to a horizon she has never seen? And to answer that, I have to ask this: why does a girl stick her thumb out on a long highway, stretching from one end of the largest island on earth to the other, and get into strangers' cars, hoping for the best? And to answer that, I have to ask this: why does a girl stand on a road at night, looking into the car with two older boys smirking at her, and choose to get in that car? Why do men, young men and old men, weave to the side of the road, lean out the window, their mouths dry with promise, and tell young girls what they think they need, trusting that fear will give them a free pass? Why might a girl say yes, when she wants to say no?

On the *Ocean Thief*, on slow days, we coiled rope. I loved the heaviness of the cord, the way my arms felt the weight of the weave, the way I had to flick and turn to make the rope lie flat. Lining the coils neatly on the upper deck; it gave me a strange pleasure. Making order, I see now: it's a pleasure that has come to distinguish many corners of my life.

Uncoiling the why, the how, of the girl I was, the dangers I stumbled into and the dangers I went looking for, is a mixed pleasure. Each length of rope leads to a new one, knotted and tangled, wet with the slime of the ocean's hidden murk.

I'd learned, by fifteen, to ask questions, to tell stories, to be entertaining. On some days, I could turn the new stepfather's mood in the right direction by unspooling the right kind of story. But these boys don't want my stories.

Tony de Ropp tells me he knows my sister, my brother. He tells me again that hitchhiking is dangerous. He tells me that this is his father's car. The boy beside him is in shadow; sitting behind him, I can see the points of his ears sticking out beyond his head, his hair crooked at the base of his neck. I don't know that boy's name; I will never know his name. Leaning across the front seat, he mutters something to Tony. The tips of their two heads become the point of a triangle, their shoulders forming the base, while his words blur into the engine's hum.

In the back seat, I take up a thread of chatter – invented anecdotes, gossip about teachers, snippets borrowed from books. When the car turns off the road, I keep talking, inventing lies, the lies that I have already learned might save me. Calm, bright-voiced, I tell the boys that I have been learning karate since my first year of high school. It's hard, I tell them, takes lots of practice, but I love it. Laughing, I tell them about the day my fictional karate instructor made the whole class sit outside for an hour, furious at the way we'd been throwing each other for laughs. I'll be going for brown belt soon. My voice is bright bright bright, but my chest begins to tighten. I ask Tony where he's going: I know the way to the bay, and this isn't it.

'A shortcut,' he says. 'We're taking a shortcut.'

I peer out of the window, squinting against the reflection of my own face. We're at the end of a street, the small box houses petering out towards the creek, the paddocks at the end of the road still undeveloped. Squashed against the window, my mouth makes puffs of condensation, little smoke signals against the glass. We drive past the last house on the street; a cheery light bleeds out from the front patio, the shadow of a family inside, gathered around the television. Then there's a judder, a lift, as the car slips off the tarmac, up over the gutter.

In the front seat, Tony de Ropp hoots, 'Yee-hah, let's go off road.'

Outside, it's just moon and stars now. The streetlights have gone, and the car is bumping, each jolt jarring my back. In the rear of the station wagon something clangs and chimes with each ditch, each turn. My hand slips into the catch on the door, and I flick the lock open. Beside Tony, the boy whose name I will never know has started whooping with him, as though he's in an advertisement for Coke or Land Rovers. The boy's hand reaches into the back, flailing around, trying to reach my leg. 'Having a good time, K.C.?'

I've seen films where people jump or fall from moving cars. They roll neatly and then lie, staring up, panting. Or they get up and run.

This is the way I like to remember it: that I push that door open, and I roll, like a brown-belted karate stuntwoman, like Supergirl, like Diana of the hunt. But all I know is this: my shoulder shoves against the door as the car slips into another ditch. There's a gut-wrenching crack, and then I am swinging on the door, my legs following my body, dragging on the mud. Inside the car, the boys are shouting. I remember to let go. I don't so much roll as scramble, my limbs sagging behind me, out of my control. The car slows as I scrabble upright and begin running to where I think the houses might be. I'm not sure. Beneath my feet, there's stubby grass, mud. Ahead, in the darkness, something that might be a low fence and, beyond that, a sprinkle of house lights. Or not house lights. Streetlights? I can't tell. I have no idea where I am. The car is idling behind me. Tony de Ropp shouts, 'We just wanted to scare you. We just wanted to teach you a lesson.'

I stop running. I screech back, 'Fuck you. You're not my teacher.'

In fact, now that I remember it, that was the night I arrived, grass-stained and battered, at Lisa O'Daniel's house to discover the little audience of teenage girls and their boyfriends she'd assembled, while she circled me, calling me *slut*, *backstabber*, *liar*. She recited it over and over, like a chant, while I tried to ask: Why? What did I do?

After a while, I stopped asking, and stood with my palms up, letting her words hammer down until the bruises bled together into their own map, a landscape of mortification.

THE LADY POLICE OFFICER has a carefully arranged kind face. She looks young, not much older than me, her tidy ponytail barely touching the top of her cotton collar, a smear of gloss on her lips. A few strands of hair have slipped out, clumping across her forehead. She keeps patting at the damp hair, smoothing it down. Her hair is the colour of hessian; it makes me think of kindergarten sack races, those joyous, chaotic events that ended up with a pile of giggling five-year-olds wriggling on the ground, puppy-like. She says, 'I'm Constable Turner. Do you need a glass of water?'

Water is not the first thing on my mind, but I nod anyway.

It's the older officer, the one who makes me think of my father, who asks most of the questions. He says, 'And you sat in the front of the taxi?'

I nod. 'Yes.'

He sighs. 'Next to the driver?'

I nod again.

He sighs again.

'And how much have you had to drink?'

Obediently, I try to do a mental calculation. 'We—'

'We?'

'Me and my friend, Penny.'

He looks around, as though expecting her to materialise beside me. Pale flesh shakes slightly on his chin as he swivels back to me. 'And where is she now?'

23

'At the party, I suppose. She – I was ready to leave. She wasn't.'

'So, you were at a party? And you left without your friend?'

I look at Constable Turner, who stares at the notepad in front of her, the pen lying across the page. The note of accusation in the sergeant's voice is clear, but I am unsure precisely what I am being accused of. Unsure whether the greater sin was leaving my friend at the party or being at the party in the first place.

'Yes,' I say, 'I told you that. I was at a party and then I wanted to go home, and I went outside, and I got a taxi.'

In another room, with a cooling cup of tea in front of him, the soft-faced man who brought me here is filling in his details. A single policeman, a young constable in his first month on the job, is taking his statement. It was another taxi that stopped; the driver got out of the car, put his hand under my elbow and guided me into the back seat. To that driver I'd said, 'Please, just take me home,' and he'd said, no, the police needed to know what had happened. They needed to stop this man. 'Most of us,' he said, 'are good guys. He gives us a bad name. Just think,' my kind rescuer said, 'just think what would happen if another girl was picked up by him. Don't you want to stop him?'

So, I am here, trying to stop him, after cowering in the back seat, head down, while this man, the driver of the second taxi, followed the first, took note of the licence plate. He did his duty for me, and now I am doing mine for all the other girls.

The sergeant asks again, 'So you were drinking before you even went to the party?'

I take a sip of water. It bubbles down my throat, sweet as air, and I keep swallowing until I have guzzled the whole glass.

'And then you kept drinking at the party?'

I try for levity. 'That's what usually happens at parties.'

He glares at me, writes something on the pad in front of

him, then looks at my little green top, at the neckline that I'd cut out with kindergarten craft scissors, the kind with zigzag shapes, to make a bigger V against my cleavage. 'How much?'

I shake my head; the room spins. 'A bottle of cider before we left. We took two bottles of wine to the party. We drank them both. But maybe some other people helped. I don't know.'

'And?'

In the same way that *I was raped* seems like the wrong sentence, focusing on the wrong person, it seems to me that the horse-faced sergeant is asking the wrong questions, of the wrong person. But I am too drunk and too bewildered to find the words. There is something tight and boiling about the uniformed man in front of me. Ready, like my father, to turn to anger. So, I am trying. I am trying to help him to help me. That's all he wants, he explains earnestly. He needs the whole picture; my statement will be used later. It matters. Everything, anything I can tell him. The whole truth. He needs the truth.

I add, 'And a glass of Benedictine.'

'Right.' He lifts his eyes to me. Waits, pen poised.

'Two glasses of Benedictine.'

He writes something else down. Rusty brown spots cover the back of his hand.

Constable Turner twists her stubby ponytail. Her fingernails are bitten, like mine. I want to like her. I really want to like her, and I desperately want her to like me.

I'm in that boxy room for over an hour, with the walls beginning to shine with condensation. Hot air presses on me, the smell of the floor polish mixing with the scent of my own fear, the smell of my own tears. I drink a cup of cold tea with three sugars. Beneath the table, my legs start to shake, small tremors shuddering up and down my thighs, like isolated electric shocks. Anger begins to bubble in my gut, and I eat it down with the plate of sugared biscuits they put in front of me.

When I've eaten all the biscuits, I move my finger across the plate, tamping the sugar and crumbs into my fingertips.

The sergeant asks patiently why I sat in the front seat of the taxi; he asks me if I always sit in the front seat of taxis. He is, he says, trying to help me; these are the questions that will be asked in court. I hadn't thought about court. I hadn't thought about anything except getting off the road, getting home, taking the next step, getting away. But now I am here, and I have already told Sid, the kind driver of the second taxi, that I will do my best to stop this man, do my best to help other girls. I say, yes, I want to pursue this. Somewhere, down in the pit of me, not completely crushed by the landslide of biscuits, the tiny worm of anger begins to flourish.

'And then he stopped the car?' Constable Turner taps her pen against the table. It's the first question she's asked, and I'm startled.

'No. He – I was asleep – I mean, sort of.'

'Beside him?'

'Sorry?'

'In the front seat. Beside him?'

'Yes.'

'Why did you fall asleep? Would you do this often in a taxi?'

I wonder, briefly, whether Constable Turner has ever gone out drinking with her girlfriends, whether she's stood on a bridge, or by a park, singing songs to the moon, feeling invincible.

She taps her pen again. 'What then?'

'Then I felt him – he – inside me.' I try to correct myself. 'Not straight away. There was – he sort of – there was some touching. I wasn't sure. I tried to move away, I guess – and something – I couldn't tell what was happening.'

She says, 'I understand this is difficult.' Her eyes lower to the pad in front of her. I realise then that she doesn't understand at all how difficult this is. That we are different kinds of young women, on different sides of the table.

I say, 'He was groping at me, I guess – I didn't know, wasn't sure what it was, just – and I tried to brush him off, I sort of didn't want to notice it. I hoped I was imagining it, or that he'd just stop, you know?'

She raises her eyebrows. 'And?'

'And then the car – I think it swerved, I don't know – and then the car – I guess we went off the road. It stopped and he—' His beard, black and damp with spit, his skin stinking above me, the peeling back of the silk of my beautiful French knickers, the push, the pull—

She says, 'You were asleep, and he put his penis inside you? He penetrated you?'

I blink slowly. Was it his penis? The word, *penis*, seems small, pink, soft. I am distracted, thinking about those two words: *penis*, *penetrate*. How close they are. The constable continues the tap-tap of the pen against the tabletop. What was *inside me*? Inside me was guts blood intestine veins pulpy masses of fat and muscle pulsing heart wet lungs. What else? A penis? A finger?

'He put something inside me. I assume it was his penis. I didn't check.' The little worm of anger lifts its head. 'He was driving a taxi and I thought I was safe. Jesus fucking Christ.' I'm trying to be careful, to remember, to feel. Was it a finger? Was it a fist? A penis? But it's awkward now, to stop, to pause, to reconsider.

The sergeant raises his eyebrows. The alcohol, the language. The lack of decorum, the excess cleavage. Everything about me, I realise, offends him.

He says, 'Are you someone who would generally tell the truth?'

I say, 'Are you asking if I'm lying? If I'm a liar?'

Constable Turner makes a shushing shape with her lips, and then she smiles. Lips closed; teeth hidden. She leans across the table, rests her hand on my wrist. Her skin is cool. She says, 'I know you're upset, but—'

Right then, I hate her. Her neat ponytail, her clean, uncreased shirt, her tapping pen. Everything about her is as repugnant to me as I am to her colleague. I hate that I am on this side of the table – the side where the trauma sits – and she is on the other.

I say, 'Fuck off. You have no idea how upset I am.' My words slur a little and the sergeant raises one grizzled eyebrow.

But the words burn, the questions burn. The sergeant has seen me for what I am: a liar, a girl with the certain knowledge that the imagined life is superior, a girl who wants to spin gold from straw.

REBECCA GARDEN introduced me to the thrill of the lie. Rebecca Garden is the most beautiful girl in kindergarten. Her slight nose upturns like a cartoon nose, the freckles trailing across it. Her hair is golden, twisted every morning into perfect ringlets.

It is that time in kindy when the birthday party has full currency. *I am inviting you to my party. I am not inviting you to my party.* Parties provide full access to games of chasies, to first dibs on the blocks in the classroom, to additional playlunch treats from other people's lunch boxes. I hear of invites being slid across the room, passed to other people. Trudi Andrews gave one to Sally Waters. Jennie Gordon handed invitations to five girls, not one of them me.

With my father smashing about the house and my mother sitting awake at the narrow melamine dining table weeping all night, there is no room in my house for parties or for lunchtime invitations. Instead, I huddle in the classroom at recess, poring over the coloured story cards and paper books, my mouth watering with the anticipation of all those words, the worlds to be unlocked.

Outside of the kindy room, we line our bags up on a brown bench, the paint thick and glossy. At this bench the simple miracle of my first party invite occurs, and it is Rebecca Garden who gives it to me. Standing alongside me she whispers, 'I am having a party.' Just as simple as that. And then: 'You are invited.'

I say, 'When is it?'

'Today,' she says. 'This afternoon.'

When the afternoon bell rings, I walk home with the bubble and hope of a party softening every step. My father is in the front yard, his white singlet streaked with brown from dirt and work. My sister holds my hand, and the whine of the lawnmower is everywhere, so we wait like that, holding hands. After a while the waiting isn't working so my sister shouts and he can't hear over the mower so then she stands right in front of him and she keeps shouting until he stops, and the front yard is so quiet it hurts my ears.

'It's a party,' my sister says. 'Down at the creek.'

'One of the creek houses?' Dad looks up fast, maybe thinking of Ted the Wrecker and why he would have a party for kids like me. But I am not going to Ted the Wrecker's house although my dad does know him because my dad knows everyone because he is the boss of the police station and that means he's the boss of Boolaroo.

She says, 'It's at the Gardens' house.'

He gives a five-dollar note to my sister, and the bubble inside me floats up through my feet and up.

We buy a family block of chocolate and a Little Golden Book, *The Saggy Baggy Elephant*, and my sister wraps them both in soft yellow tissue paper. It's a hot day, the beginning of summer, and the creek is murky green down the back of Boolaroo. We pass Ted the Wrecker's and we cross over the narrow bridge and then we are in the single street that makes up Cockle Creek and I hold my breath with the excitement of it, using ordinary words to keep myself on the ground. *Bait*, I think, spelling it out in my head. And: *Prawn. Walking. Toast.* Only when we are closer to the few houses that are in Cockle Creek, only then do I let myself have other words: *Party. Pure. Golden.*

Cockle Creek is darker than Boolaroo. The houses in this small row are all made of wood or fibro, with wire fences. The house with the number that Rebecca Garden has given me has a couch on the front porch, its green upholstery torn and battered. A mystery, I think, to have an outside couch, and I linger over the word *mystery*. My sister takes a breath so deep I see her lungs expand. I feel her hand take mine, and we step through the gate. It's clear there are no other children here yet, so my offering will be received in special glory.

We knock, and Rebecca Garden's mother comes to the door. Her bum is so wide that she has to stand sideways to get through the door onto the step. She looks down at me, with my yellow-wrapped present, and her face slides sideways to my sister, who, squeezing my hand, looks up at Rebecca Garden's mother and says, 'She's here for the party.'

'Party?'

I whisper, 'It's a party. For Rebecca. It's her birthday.'

The wide-bummed woman looks right at me then. 'Her birthday isn't until August.'

I think of some other words quick-smart. *Lickety-split*, I think. *Tickety-boo*.

I say, 'It's today. Actually.'

We wait while Rebecca Garden's mother slams the screen door and lumbers back into the darkness of the house. When she comes back out, she has Rebecca Garden attached to her hip, clinging behind her, and she has a wooden spoon in her other hand. She says, 'I will give her a thrashing, the little liar.' Rebecca looks at her feet, in her little cross sandals, dirt blotting around them, and then she looks back up to me, her face a sharp pink. My stomach twists. It was so stupid of me. So horribly stupidly stupid to think there was a party, to have got it so stupidly wrong. And with my sister there, watching. Everything is shadowy now, dark. A cloud moves over Cockle

31

Creek and Boolaroo and Rebecca Garden's hair is mousy brown, not blonde. Her fat mother says, 'She'll be getting the wooden spoon, that's for sure.' I can't say anything, not a word to Rebecca. When the door closes, I can hear her wailing.

All the way home my sister and I are silent, walking along the dirt road to First Street. Our feet plap and slap on the road, my throat clogs with the red dirt from it, my face smudged with red so that you can't tell where I am burning and where I am dust.

My father is still mowing the lawn, his singlet speckled with the frightening bits of grass that fly up and sting. He doesn't look up as we walk in the gate. My sister gives me the Little Golden Book and one row of the chocolate. The rest, she says, is for her to share with the other sisters. The chocolate has three different flavours in it: caramel, coconut ice, Turkish delight. The Turkish delight is disgusting, so I throw my half-sucked square of that in the bin. The others I eat before dinner, while I crouch over the story of the Saggy Baggy Elephant, who never feels properly dressed, who never feels let in.

Rebecca Garden is not at school the next day, or the day after that, and then it is the weekend, when I sit outside and watch my father circling the horses in the paddock. When she comes back to school her hair is not in ringlets, it is tied back into plain pigtails. We don't look at each other, we don't share, we don't speak. I only see the circle of bruising on her arm when Miss Noble makes her draw a letter R for Rebecca on the blackboard. The chalk makes a rattle on the board and I think: R is for *rescue* and *rotund* and *rabbit* and *rather*. My mouth waters at the thought of the word *rotund* and I say it to myself all morning. Rotund. Rotund. Rotund.

But the thrill of the lie, the glory of it: this I hold to myself, nursing it like a water bottle, warm against my belly. *Audacity* is a word I learn later, the next year, when my sister is caught out with a boy. The audacity of Rebecca Garden's lie pleases me. The courage of it. It's a lie that says: I will not be the poor girl at the creek with no party and no money and no friends. I will be someone else.

It's a lie that says: Fuck you. This is not straw. It is gold.

Although I do not learn that word until I am seven, when the older boy next door invites me over and asks politely if I would like to fuck.

WINTER ARRIVED IN Sydney after the trial, as though signifying the end of something greater than a single season. The trial, the turns within it, marked the end of me. Or at least, the end of this version of myself. It was as though I'd burned, or drowned, the girl who kicked her heels hopefully at that party. After, I was wet with the sopping sense of shame it left in its wake, and sore with the sealing-up of my words. I would not speak of this, I swore, not again, not after all those words battering me in that dusty courtroom.

Rain sheeted down on the last day, sudden and brutal the way Sydney rains are, leaving oil-slicked puddles across the roads and footpaths. Water dripped from shoes, hair, coats. Darkness dropped down early, an abrupt, dusk-free curtain tightly drawn, denoting the last stage of autumn. When I left the courthouse, I untied my hair from the tight bun I'd scraped it into and walked through the rain until my clothes clung to me like plastic wrap to a sausage. I felt as though I'd been compressed and minced, pulped in a machine. Churned through. I had no hat, no raincoat, no umbrella, and I let the water pound on my head, dripping down my back. If it hailed, I didn't feel it. I couldn't tell if it was warm or cold, could barely hear the traffic I stepped dully into, hardly blinked at the driver who tooted his horn at me, shouting that I'd get myself killed. Water seeped into my shoes and I nodded, held my hand up in a salute and kept walking. Droplets spattered with each step

34

until my shoes were sodden, leaving black stripes across my feet when I peeled my tights off that night, shivering with a chill so deep I was sure that my bones were frozen.

In the weeks after that the cold of winter set in properly, and I met it with the warmth of vodka and strangers, lots of strangers. Friends of friends of friends, or men I met in loud nightclubs, shouting over Cyndi Lauper. Anyone who could keep the babble out of my head.

I had no feelings about the man whose sperm made the beginnings of the baby. Shooting Soldiers: that was the name of his band. I kid you not. Naturally, he played bass. Paper blinds crinkled against the window of my share-house bedroom, the tears patched with coloured tape. The bass player paused at the door of the room, staring in astonishment at the lack of floor space. Every surface was covered with crumpled clothes, CDs, batches of papers and books. On the floor, my mattress – I couldn't afford a bed base – swam beneath this surface of chaos, and to get into bed at night I kicked the pile aside, huddling deep down into the covers and pretending not to notice the encroaching pile surrounding me.

The bass player suggested we turn the light out so that he didn't have to look at the mess. I'd spent my life working on that principle, so it seemed perfectly acceptable to me. He didn't use a condom. I didn't ask him to.

Somewhere underneath the Vesuvius of clothing and books and assorted detritus, somewhere in there a pill packet floated. Sometimes I remembered to dig it out. Sometimes I did not.

When I woke up in the morning, he was gone. But he'd left me a little gift.

The clinic sat at the intersection of two busy roads. Friendly white doors, with the word *Preterm* written in a cheerful orange arc. When the door opened the word broke in two: *Pre. Term*. Sylvie came with me, the same way I'd gone with her three years earlier, when David Fox failed to put on the condom he'd promised to use. It was, he explained, different for a man. He was twenty-three, a man to Sylvie's seventeen-year-old girl. We took the day off school and caught the 5 a.m. train into Sydney, staring out the window at the sun burning over the sandstone of the Hawkesbury River. Every so often we burst out, *It's different for a man*, and folded over in desperate, sad laughter. By the time we got to Sydney, we'd worn the catchphrase thin and our laughter sounded only sad.

Sylvie, like Lisa O'Daniel, was one of the pretty girls. In high school, she sat on the beach nursing Chiko rolls for surfing boyfriends, her thin brown legs stretched out before her. At fifteen, we planned to run away together to Byron Bay, until her mother offered to buy her a new surfboard if she stayed. At school, we competed for first place, checking our grades against each other's. When Mr King took me aside after our yearly exams and said, 'You are the smartest girl in the school, full stop. Now stop wasting your talents, Kacey,' I asked, 'Smarter than Sylvie?'

Mr King touched my ponytail – I'd wound curling ribbon in it, so that I looked like a Christmas gift – and said again, 'Stop wasting your talents.' He rested his hand on my shoulder, pressing it so that his fingers pointed down, just touching the trim of my bra. Through the thin cotton of my school blouse, he lifted the bra strap lightly, absent-mindedly. I heard, many years later, that he'd married an ex-student. Strange, the way things work out.

Sylvie fell in love with David Fox. Or, she thought she might be in love with him. Could try to be. Until he lied about the condom and we made our pre-dawn trip to Sydney, to the Preterm Clinic.

And then, three years later, it was my turn. It was louder than I'd expected, the machine gagging, a chugging engine roar as though a tractor drove through my gut, razing everything, me included. Afterwards, I sat in the waiting room reading the pamphlets and eating soft sliced cheese on Sao crackers. My hand kept going to the crackers, my mouth kept opening, I kept eating until the red plastic plate was empty of everything but crumbs.

I always thought it was a girl.

If I'd kept her, I would have named her Tabitha.

IT WAS SYLVIE'S IDEA to leave. She was always courageous. In our last year of school, not long after David Fox's little sperm wriggled its way to Sylvie's egg, she caught the train home from the city one night and walked home along the wooded cycle path. Halfway there, she heard footsteps coming closer behind her, crunching on the dirt. She started to walk faster – not to make a big deal of it, if there was a stranger minding his own business, just escalating her pace a little. The pace of the footsteps following escalated too. She tried to say this to herself: *It's okay. I'm overreacting. It's someone having a joke.* Because this is what you learn to do, when you are a girl walking alone. Try to stay calm but be ready to run. Like walking past wild animals, we train ourselves: *Stay calm, keep your distance, don't make him mad.*

She only started sprinting, her heart burning, when she could hear the running behind her.

The stranger behind Sylvie wrapped his arm across her chest, just below her throat. With her back pressed against him, she could feel how tall he was. His hand rested at the nape of her neck which, he promised, he would break if she struggled. She did not struggle. Afterwards, she walked home, crying, and told no one what had happened. For months after, she didn't answer the phone. On weekends, she said she was busy, didn't want to go out, wanted to be left alone. After the trial of the taxi driver, the trial where I was not, allegedly, on trial, I stopped answering my own phone. That was when Sylvie told me what had happened to her.

I sat beside her on a bench outside the Hopetoun Hotel, a bottle of cider in my hand. 'Why didn't you tell me? Why didn't you talk about it?'

She snorted, lifting her head slightly. 'Right. Like talking about it worked out so well for you.'

I opened my mouth, then shut it again.

She took a swig of her cider, wiping her mouth with her sleeve. 'Anyway, it happens to girls all the time. If we talked about it every time some dick moved on us, we'd never shut up. There'd be no space for anything else.'

Peeling green paint covered the metal bench. Some of the paint flecks stuck to my bare legs. Sylvie stared out at the sweeping traffic and she said, 'You should just go. Go as far away as you can.' Her hand slipped into mine. We had that sort of friendship: hand-holding, heads leaning close, whispering. 'Everything,' she said, 'has turned to shit.'

I shook my head and said, 'I've got nowhere to go.' I had no means, no plan, no way.

She said, 'Get off this bloody land. Go *somewhere*.' She peered at me. 'Look at you. You're a mess.'

I patted at my hair, tried to wipe the smears from under my eyes.

'No. God, not your make-up. You're a mess emotionally. You need to get out of this hole.'

I grinned, then, opening my arms wide to the Surry Hills traffic, sang the refrain from 'We Gotta Get Out of This Place'.

She was still staring into the traffic. 'Yes,' she said. 'We do.' Then: 'Come to India with me. Let's go to India.'

I said, 'How? I've got no money. Neither have you. How would we get to India?'

She said, 'My mother will help. Maybe – ' her voice less sure here ' – maybe she'll help you too.'

Although I said, 'Don't be ridiculous, why would she help me?' I had a tiny flame of hope. Maybe I could escape, make some cash somehow, get on a plane and get off this giant island. Be somewhere else, be someone else. Don Quixote, tripping through the world, questing, adventuring, making himself the knight of knights.

But Sylvie's mother could not help me. So only one of us went to India.

I caught the bus to the airport to see her off. She cashed in the first of her traveller's cheques and we drank Bloody Marys in the airport bar, ticking off memories until her final boarding call. We clung to each other like lovers, crying until we hiccupped, and the airline assistant said it was time to go and we swore undying love to each other as though we were in a movie.

After Sylvie left for India, for a new exotic life, I stared at maps of the world and got fired from one waitressing job after another until my flatmates left me a note letting me know they'd had a vote and it was time for me to leave. I looked at the map pinned to the living room wall – a 1940s etching of Australia, fringed by the islands of the Pacific – and I traced my finger along the threshold of the land. How far would be far enough? How far, I wondered, would I have to travel to get away from myself and the stench of my own failures? I flattened my hand against the pale blue surrounding the continent, wishing myself into the depth of it, and wondered what it would take to burn everything behind me.

I BOUGHT THE backpack from an English girl, a friend of a friend. 'Broome,' she said. 'That's where you need to go. That will heal you, darlin'.' The dropped 'g' on darling was an affectation, I thought, as though she'd heard the phrase spoken in an old American film – probably by Elizabeth Taylor playing Southern – and used it whenever the opportunity came up. She hugged me after that, held me so close that my nose bent sideways against her cheek; I could see a glob of golden wax, curled like a foetus inside her ear. She said, 'You poor thing.' The friend who'd introduced us, a girl from drama school, looked at her feet, clasping her hands at her crotch, an external chastity belt. I'm sure she didn't realise the implication. I'm sure she didn't realise, either, that my troubles were private, mine to tell.

Although when you've stood in a courtroom talking about your knickers and your sexual habits, your sense of privacy does get a little distorted.

I turned up at Mitch's house wearing my new jeans, so tight I had to lie on the bed and wriggle into them. Heavy black lace-ups, a fake leather jacket. The army-green, externally framed pack dug into the muscles on my back. Mitch was the boy I'd loved in high school, the boy who had no interest in me but who took pleasure in my interest in him. The boy who played me. I couldn't get enough of him. The jeans were for him. I wanted him to notice, to wish I wouldn't go, to make promises to me. But I was going, whatever he said, however much he begged.

He said nothing. He did not beg.

He offered me a ride up the coast on the back of his motor-bike.

Newcastle, New South Wales. Only two hours up the high-way, but two hours closer to the end of the country, two hours closer to escape. Everything there is borrowed or stolen. The name itself was taken from the northern English city that marks a shift from the low hills of Northumbria to the peaks of Scotland, obliterating the original name – Muloobinba – as though the Worimi had never been there. Even the name of the state – New South Wales – is a reminder of Welsh miners who could see only the dull grey-green that defines the interior, blinking against the luminous-yellow sandstone, unable to see what was before them, what had been taken. It does not resemble slate-grey quarries and the wanton green of Wales, but those long-gone men could see only the absence of their own country, a life of *hiraeth* – the longing for home – stretching ahead of them.

My own longing was unspoken and endless. I clung to Mitch, letting my helmet rest against his leather-clad back. I wrapped my arms around him and pretended he loved me. *Dolly* magazine had photo shoots of girls on the back of motorbikes, hands on the riders' waists, never on the handlebars. I could be one of those girls. Wind on my face. On the road, baby! Fucking Kerouac. I could be one of *his* girls.

Outside of Newcastle, I leaned into Mitch as we turned onto a ring road. My pack was heavy on my shoulders and I shrugged slightly to ease the pain of it. Perhaps the road was wet. Perhaps a car in front slowed down. Perhaps I leaned back, losing balance, changing the weight on the bike. Only this is clear: the crack of the tarmac, the shred of skin, the tumble of sky-black-sky-wheel-grass. My pack bouncing under me, proving on the downward turn a landing pillow, and on the upward turn a weight against me. I landed on the grass verge, arms still in my pack, skin shredded. Above me, a woman's face. 'Can you hear me?'

I heard her but I couldn't answer. Instead I shouted Mitch's name again and again, unable to understand where I was, what had happened. Somehow, there was an ambulance. Now, years later, I cannot think how it came to be there. We travelled without mobile phones, then. Someone in one of the houses, I suppose. A driver running, worried, losing breath, hammering on the door of a house, asking to use the phone. Pointing back at the road, at the cars slowing as the drivers carefully steered around the prone motorbike, the two figures lying on the grass, the small audience.

Later, in the hospital, I wore a starched cotton gown. Mitch came to visit, showing me the patch of skin that came from his hand, the only injury on him. I couldn't walk. White sheets scratched beneath my skin; my toes, painted a cheerful celebratory red, poked out at the bottom. I asked one of the nurse's aides to untuck the bottom of the sheets: 'Please,' I said, 'I feel so stuck, I feel like I'm in prison, like I'll never escape.' I'd started crying, big hiccupping tears, saying it again: 'I'll never escape. I'll never get out of here.'

The aide was young and wide, skin folding over her elbows, over her neck. Even her hands, as she lifted the sheet from the end of the bed, seemed padded. I'd spent the weeks leading up to the trial not eating, counting calories the way I did in high school, contemptuous of those who needed to eat. After the verdict, I went to a Chinese restaurant and ate two servings of deep-fried honey king prawns. Honey and oil slicked across my face, my hands, down the front of my specially-purchased-to-look-like-you-might-be-a-public-servant cover-up dress.

Mitch left me the dried piece of skin from his hand. It was the size of his palm, tightened into an opaque circle. I held it over my own hand until the nurse came. She pursed her lips at me, with my red toes, the shred of an indifferent man's hand sitting in my own palm. She said, 'We had to cut your jeans off you, they were so tight.' She flicked a glance at my arms, round, unmuscled. 'No one needs to wear jeans that tight.'

Shame, that familiar flame, burned beneath my skin. It was always there, waiting for a word, a look, a breath, to fan it back to life. My constant companion, my night-light, my day-shadow. The year before I'd read Blake, sitting in a café, holding the book up high in hopes of an audience, peering at the pages. If mercy was the human dress, shame was both my underwear and my overcoat. Disgust drifted down from the nurse's face, sprinkling like dandruff onto my neat hospital sheets. I was too fat, too needy, too young, too me.

She huffed slightly as she sat me up and tightened the starched gown around my waist. The aide with the blonde hair and the lipstick and the cascading flesh wheeled a chair over to the bed. Deep orange lipstick made a lightning stripe on her teeth when she smiled. They stood on either side of me, their hands under my arms, while I wriggled to the brink of the bed, my feet dangling below me. My red toes seemed impossibly far away; the bed seemed ridiculously, unnecessarily high. Underneath my arm, in the soft part, the nurse pressed her hand.

'Please,' I said. 'Your ring, it's hurting me.'

'I can't take my ring off for you. Come on, Kacey. The more you fuss, the longer it will take.' She nodded to the blonde aide, and the two of them heaved and hefted, lifting me down from the bed and into the chair. The aide made a guttural grunt as she lifted. They had to turn me around once my feet touched the floor, and for some reason I couldn't remember how my feet worked, how to make them turn, how to make my body obey my commands. It wasn't the first time that my body had been frozen, not the first time that I failed to make my limbs work.

They shuffled, the two of them, with a bit of grunting and a bit of sighing, until I was turned, butt facing chair. Cold tiles scorched my feet as I lowered myself into the chair. There was a pause, almost musical, a suspension, while the nurse gave a glance around the empty ward, and then the aide began to push.

Inside the X-ray room, the smell of polish filled each corner, thick and solid as lard. The nurse and the aide laid me down on the sheets, scratchy white but with the smell of clean. I thought of the night the bass player came to my room, the crumpled sheets, grey with unwash, dribbling onto the floor, fluted like sand dunes. I thought of the earlier night, too, returning to that room as the sun came up, my mouth dry, my make-up smeared like a smack across my face, a sheaf of Helpline pamphlets creased in my hand.

In the hospital, though, it was a relief to lie on those clean sheets, to feel the cool hands on my arms, my hips, my face. I don't remember the X-ray. I imagine it like a film, a cancer film, with me staring up into the white column as I slide through with a musical accompaniment: something choral, something magnificent. Arvo Pärt perhaps. But Arvo Pärt, and magnificent choral music, is from my life later, from the life where I know such things, where I do not mispronounce Somerset Maugham, where I am not daunted by boys with too much money and not enough manners. Magnificence, yes, this comes later, like the colours busting from black.

In that room, there was just this:

The shutter whirr of the machine, the slicing light travelling the length of my body. I thought about my rolls of fat, the thickness of my hips. I wondered if the doctors would see the fat on the negative of my body, if they would gather, pointing, pretending to themselves and to each other that they were not disgusted.

The radiograph showed a small crack on the bone at the base of my back, my coccyx. The doctor who told me this was red-haired, with muscled arms. Freckles smattered on his nose. Watching his mouth move as he told me about this bone in my lower back – my bum bone, I thought of it – I imagined him as a boy, when his muscles were not developed, when his red hair was ungroomed, his freckles broader, redder. His mouth kept moving. *Light fracture. Stress point.*

The bone that holds me together.

I turned my head from him. Shadows formed shapes on the wall; I could see flickers of green outside, glimpses of leaves lifting in the wind. The light grew longer, and the red-headed doctor kept talking about hairline fractures, but I knew I was already broken. While the light flickered and arched against the dull green wall, I tried to form words in my head. I tried to craft a promise.

In primary school, I found an abridged and illustrated retelling of *Don Quixote*. The illustrations were watercolours, soft pastels bleeding out onto the page, the paper thick with a rich inky smell. At lunchtimes I sat in the corner of the temporary classroom that permanently housed the school library, and I breathed in the smell of the ink, gazing at the pearly colours. In that hospital room, instead of seeing the shadowy green against the wall when I closed my eyes, I saw the thick pages, the cream faux-leather cover of *Don Quixote*. And, inside, the sketch of Don Quixote, a long skinny man with a drooping moustache dragging an unwilling horse out from the stable. In the illustration, the surrounding hills are painted a dusky mauve, and the horse's spine droops in the middle like a badly tied hammock. On the ground, a pile of battered, rusty armour rests at the horse's feet and the text below the picture says: *Rocinante. Formerly an ordinary horse.* In that grey demountable building, I breathed those words in, the possibility of them, chewing on them like cud: *formerly ordinary*.

Beneath my green hospital gown, the vinyl of the chair was cool. Near the top of my thigh, there was a slice in the seat, as though another occupant had dug at it with a nail file, or a knife, in an expression of desperation. An escape plan, hatched under pressure, badly thought out. My own nails worried at the upholstery flap, lifting it up and down, scraping at the velvety underside.

The red-headed doctor asked me to stand, to put the weight on my feet. Cool tiles pressed against my soles; my hands were tight against his forearms. His muscles flexed beneath my palms. 'Okay?' he said, and slowly released his hand, stepping back so that I stood without support, still reaching out for him.

The blindness came suddenly, in a terrible rush. With one breath, the world, the floor, the faces all disappeared while my hands thrashed about in dark air. It didn't descend. It didn't rain down on me, or close like a curtain. It was there, everywhere, as though it had always been there. Instead of the doctor, there was darkness. Instead of the nurse, there was darkness. Where the walls were, where the green shone bright against the shadows: darkness.

In kindy, we painted with glorious blobs of colour, squirted them across the page from plastic bottles: red sliding like blood, yellow as vivid as a cartoon. The magic came when we folded the page, rubbing each side together. Behold! A twin-sided multicolour. Mrs Noble pegged the paintings out on the school porch, and we watched the bright colours flap in the sun. The next morning we painted over the glorious twin blobs in black, covering the whole page, mystified by her gleeful instructions. The black dried quickly and, when it did, she gave us knitting needles with which we could scratch the picture. Underneath the black, the bright colours lurked, ready to burst out in radioactive squiggles, codes, secret messages.

In that curtained hospital room, I understood that it was the other way around. I understood that the black waited beneath the bright.

My sight went as quickly as that sentence, as quickly as a breath, and without it I had no sense of my own body in space. Without light, without sight, I could not measure distance, could not measure the feeling of my own legs, my own feet, my own arms. I floated in darkness, fell in nothingness. Someone shouted. My own voice, disconnected. I could barely make sense of my own words. Terror rose up, so swiftly, so fiercely. Other voices, not mine, joined the shouting. Hands gripped my arms, nails slicing into my skin. Voices. Without faces, without sight, I couldn't understand distance – were they shouting at me from the other side of the room? From next to me? From space, where they floated, bodyless and faceless?

'Calm down,' one of the voices intoned. 'Calm down, Kacey.' She sounded out the syllables of my name, slowly. Kay. Cee. Calm. Down.

I've never thought of myself as an especially visual person. Often, I wander through the world slightly oblivious to what surrounds me, I am so immersed in my own thoughts. But without sight I was lost. I could not find my footing, I could not stand, was sure I was falling. And falling not just to the floor; falling through space. Perhaps even through time.

I could hear them shouting back at me, instructing me: *it's there, just stop, breathe, the chair is behind you, hold your hand out.* But where was my hand? Which bit of me was my hand? Without sight, even the word – *hand* – seemed meaningless. Hand. What is it? Somehow, I flapped it, flailing wildly.

Someone – the nurse? – grasped it, clasped my palm against hers. Something brushed against my arm and I felt my body lower, felt the solidity of the wheelchair beneath me.

Now, I look back at her, this shouting creature, her thrashing arms, her panic tumbling, and the metaphor is so obvious as to be ridiculous, like those dreams that are hilarious in their lack of subtlety. I had one recently where I was juggling too many plates, terrified they would smash. And there she is: this twenty-year-old me, pummelling the air, terrified of all the things she does not wish to see, all the things she must make herself blind to, simply to survive.

Hysterical blindness. That's what they called it. Perhaps men, boys, could go blind in this way too. But it would be girlish, womanish, of them to do so.

But whatever those voices intoned, they were wrong. Calm was not what I needed to be. Not then.

I LOST COUNT OF the days in hospital, but it can't have been more than five. Crisp starched sheets held me above and below, so tight that it felt like I was stitched in. During those days when I could not see, I was pliable, letting the nurses manoeuvre me upright, my muscles softer than the sheets. Holding my hand, showering me; I could only feel their kindness then. Later, they would bring me back to my bed, my feet shuffling carefully on the ground, my head angled forwards so I wouldn't fall. Some mornings I could feel the brush of air against my bum where the gown was tied too loosely. I let the nurses and aides guide my hand to spoon mashed potato into my mouth, as though I were a soldier, returned from the war with shell shock. And it was a kind of shell shock, what I had, though my war was fought with fewer battalions.

I waited, and I waited, until the empty dark felt normal and I was not afraid. I waited, and I waited, until I felt again the comfort of the empty page, until I returned to neutral. And then, out of nowhere and without fanfare, I could see again. I woke in the hospital bed one morning to the creak of the trolley being wheeled across the tiled floor. Eyes closed, I counted the seconds, listening to each rotation of the double wheels, squeaking gently up and down the ward. Something chimed far away, a low sweet note, perhaps in another ward, and, without thinking about it, I opened my eyes to the light.

For a second, the return of sight was as frightening as its loss and I contemplated turning over, face to the wall, and pretending that I still couldn't see.

I understood that I had made myself blind. The diagnosis 'hysterical blindness' was there, in black ink, on the hospital reports; it was there in the discussions with the slightly bored doctor who stood at the end of the bed. Blindness, then, was something I'd invented, one more story in my ever-growing catalogue of stories, distortions and lies. Yet another thing that was, essentially, my fault.

I believed that story, and I carried it with me.

Recently I heard an actor on a talk show, a male actor, speak about going blind suddenly. He leaned back in the chair, his thin arms making circles in the air as he recounted trying to learn how to skate, which culminated in him tumbling arse first onto the ice and smashing his coccyx. He smiled at the audience, slightly sheepish as though he realised belatedly that his punchline was a little low on laughs. 'And as a result,' he said, 'I went blind.' The host laughed awkwardly, and the actor followed up with a punchier anecdote. How strange that a blow to the coccyx would result in temporary blindness.

After the motorbike crash, my coccyx had – has – a hairline crack at its tip.

Neither hysterical nor invented, after all. Just the body responding to a blow. Blindness is a natural response to trauma.

For five days, I lay in darkness and fear. I had been blind long before then. I'd chosen men who were dangerous, failed to see the risks. I'd stumbled from one bad choice to another, though not all my disasters were of my own making. I was blind, but in that room, cocooned in darkness, something opened in me.

On the lids of my eyes, there were no shapes, no pictures, no electrifying images of colour bursting through. There was only emptiness, a dark blank page, unwritten. In that hospital bed, with my sight gone and only the sound of scuffling shoes, of shushing and the whisper of wind outside, right there I decided that I did not want it, that story I was in. Not that one, my birthright, the story in which I drifted, flotsam, penniless, hopeless. Lying there, I decided I would make a different story. I would write on the blank page and make it new.

BEFORE MY MOTHER left my father, we had a prison in our backyard. A lock-up in which the drunks or vandals sobered up, lacing their fingers through the bars, singing mournful renditions of Johnny Cash songs while I sat on the back step with my cat Whiskey on my lap, listening to the singing.

Each day after school, I dawdled home alone, scuffing my feet, chatting to the sky or to myself. When there were prisoners in the lock-up, my mother cooked for them – beans, eggs, toast, bacon – sending the food out on enamel plates. Prisoners' plates, we called them. Prisoners' spoons were the silver ones. Battered, slightly misshapen through years of use, but gratifyingly heavy. My father would rap on the lock-up door as he strode past, his arms loose, his chest puffed out. I never saw the prisoners when they got out; I only heard them, or saw their hands emerging through the bars at the top of the white wooden door. They might have been formless men for all I knew – strange creatures made of hands, singing soulful drunken songs, faces pressed into stripes through the bars. Long noses, eyes peering out. Sometimes a voice not just singing but speaking, too: 'Little girl, are you the little girl who lives here? Did you go to school today?'

School has yellow and pink counting sticks. Pink equals the number four, yellow equals five and you put them next to each other to make nine. The sticks leave coloured smudges on my skin and they are magnificent. But the real magnificence is in the corner of the classroom: a box of thick cards in a lidded box. Inked in different colours, each card has a story. Red cards have big baby print and stories that aren't even stories: the duck went to the pond, the duck got lost, the mother duck came and got the duck. At the back of the box the cards are sparkling silver and golden, the print small, the depth of story dense. For treats at recess I am allowed to sit by the box, taking the cards out and running my finger across the words, tying myself into the story.

Our house is not a house of books, but in the second term of kindergarten Mrs Noble declares me *unusually clever* in a whispered conversation with my mother and begins sending home small parcels of books. Holding them in my hand, my fingers moving across the shiny pages, my mouth watering; it is better than watching the story time on *Play School*, when the turning of the pages fills me with an urgent longing.

In the afternoons, I collect the empty bottles of fizzy drink from the police station next to the house and at the back of the cool-room. In his dark uniform with the sergeant's stripes, my father seems like a different man from the one roaring through the house at night. Bluff and cheerful, his big-man voice calling me Blossom, calling my brother his little mate, as though he did not throw my mother against the wall the night before. At the back of the station, they keep crates of empty soft drink bottles: Fanta, Coke and Cherry Cheer. Sometimes the smell of the sticky sweet drink fills the back room so that my mouth waters, desperate for the liquid sugar, the pure pleasure of bubbles. Instead, we are allowed, my brother and I, to take the empty bottles to the corner shop, trading them in at the rate of five cents for every empty bottle.

We split the money, counting out carefully at the shop counter, making piles of five-cent coins. With his share, my brother buys models of old Spitfires and miniature tubs of enamel paint, then spends hours leaning over them, piecing them together, his hand steady, his gaze unwavering. Me, I take my earnings to the St Vincent de Paul charity shop on the main street. There, I tip the coins onto the counter in exchange for collections of books boxed in old fruit crates, with handwritten labels on the top: *Chldrns Assorted.* I found the first box by accident – pressing my nose into the rich papery smell, my mouth watering – when I had to wait while one of the sisters looked for a sparkly belt for a fancy-dress party. Sometimes, before I get home, I squat on the footpath, extracting book after book, greedily opening the flyleaf to see what I've got. *Maisie of the Upper Sixth. The Girl from the Bush. He Loved Her Tenderly. Pansy Goes to School. The Good Twins.* There is no sorting system, just a riveting assortment of words, of other places to be.

Everything in my world needs words to give it form; the world can be contained by words, can be measured and bound up. If I can find the right words, the formless terrors that hound me can be shrunk to a proper size. Named by me, therefore smaller than me.

Everything in these boxes is mine, the slightly damp smell of paper and ink filling my bedroom where I open them one by one, ready to disappear. The Good Twins, it turns out, aren't good at all, but terribly naughty! Children escape from robbers and from explosions and Pansy does indeed go to school, where she learns to be kinder to strangers as well as to herself. The Girl from the Bush is an Australian girl found at a train station in England after her guardian fails to collect her. Taken to the local boarding school, she works hard and learns hard and discovers her mettle and she changes into a rowing, award-winning dynamo. *Mettle*. I roll the word over my tongue, wondering where I might find mine. England, perhaps. At night, I lie awake in my bunk, planning my escape from all possible worlds, trying to find my mettle.

The Crocodile Book is the best of the charity shop books: a thick, cloth-bound annual, plump with stories and illustrations. Talking animals, runaway children, ballrooms hidden in deep forests, girls escaping shapeshifting demons. I hold the book to my face, breathing in its old pages, and I read again and again the story (clearly the best in the book) about the girl who runs away from a dark house in the woods and builds a castle from the bones of her enemies and she lives there on her own, watching the swans on the lake nearby, needing nothing but the company of the stars and the swans and the moon.

In second class, Debra Wales comes to our school. She has a deep voice that makes her sound smart, and her father is a Methodist minister, broad-backed and with a permanent grin, like a boy. All of them, her whole family, have red hair: both the mother and the father, the older sister, and Debra herself. Hers comes in the form of long red plaits, like Pippi Longstocking, and her house has books along one wall and the kitchen is full of the smell of baking and you can sit at the table while her mother gives you a glass of strawberry Quik and a piece of peppermint or cherry slice that she baked herself and then she will tell you to run along outside and play. It is like being in a book: *Milly Molly Mandy*, for instance, or *The Magic Faraway Tree* before the children go to the woods, when Mother is telling them to take care.

Debra Wales's house does not have a prison or a paddock for horses, nor does it have shouting and hitting. Even so, at lunchtime Debra pretends to be running away from home with me and Sally Waters. More than anything, I want to be friends with Debra Wales; I want to spend weekends at her house and have sleepovers in the holidays. And so I offer her my most precious gift.

I wrap *The Crocodile Book* in golden cellophane paper, bought from the newsagents with my bottle earnings, and present it to Debra Wales ceremoniously during a morning recess at school. Mrs Scott is on playground duty, her black hair whipping over one eye so that she looks like a monster. Mrs Scott has the shoutiest voice. In first class, we heard her shrieking at her children in second class, and we each whispered our hope that she would die or leave Boolaroo Public School before it was our turn to be in her class. But she did neither and now she is my teacher.

Light reflects off the golden cellophane, and it crinkles like potato crisps, but it is the book inside that makes my mouth water. I hand it to Debra while we stand outside the washroom, under the watchful eye of Mrs Scott, who peers across at her, calling, 'Is it your birthday, Debra?'

'No.'

'Then why the gift?'

Debra looks at me blankly, one shoulder lifting in an indifferent shrug. 'I don't know.' But she takes the book and folds the cellophane into a little square, slipping it into her pocket.

I wait that day and the next for Debra to tell me how much she loves the book. I wait for her to rush to school after reading the story about the castle made from enemy bones. I can barely contain the potential thrill of having someone with whom to discuss the finer points of the castle. But each day Debra arrives at school with her clean white socks up to her knees, and her neat red plaits, and her shiny school port, and she says nothing about the castle or the lake, and she does not invite me to her house for the weekend. After two weeks, I ask her to name her favourite story and she shrugs again, this time with both shoulders, so that her plaits bounce slightly against her plaid collar. She says, 'Don't know.'

Breath held, I ask which ones she's read. And again, she shrugs.

And that shrug is the truth. Debra Wales doesn't care about that book or those stories. Because the truth is this: if you don't have a prison in your backyard, you don't need to find the rules for escape.

KEROUAC HAD a lot to answer for. My thumb, pointed towards the highway, for one. Also, my legs aching from the weight of the stupidly large second-hand backpack, my mind fizzing and bubbling with so much unsaid, the hospital a shadow behind me.

Heat throbbed against my feet, ran up my calves and my thighs, turned to liquid. My pack tugged heavily on my back, the trainers suspended from it bouncing every so often against my legs. The bottom section was jammed full of books – including *On the Road*, of course, but also *Steppenwolf*, *The Unbearable Lightness of Being* and a fat collection of F. Scott Fitzgerald's mediocre short stories, *The Price Was High*. It was indeed. Perhaps this particular idea came first from Kerouac: a thumb outstretched, me on the road, a load of lies in my head. But Kerouac's girls were ciphers, receptacles for the dreams and visions of the wild young men driving and dodging through their big land, knowing the world would shift shape for them, that they would make the world change. For the girls, the world does not shift shape. For the girls, the shape that must shift is their own.

I tried to make myself the right shape. I tried to shift myself, to be the kind of girl who fits, bending myself around the world, squeezing into corners, making myself thinner than I was, trying to be less hungry, less angry. I tried to be the kind of girl

Kerouac or one of the other Great Legends might write about. But I was not that girl.

Eight fat books weighed my pack down, all of them with grand stories, one way or another, of escape. All of them with young men striding through the world wielding swords or cars or horses or girls as weapons. I searched for myself in their pages, tried to build my muscle to make myself the hero I could see there. Nonetheless, I stepped out into my own map. The great north, the wild unknown – that would save me. My vision was clear. I would be Kerouac; I would be Joyce and Thomas. Unbound on the road, I would escape, and I would find myself. Or I would be found by someone else.

My sleeping bag had a hole burned in the bottom of it after my encounter with the hairy driver. He'd picked me up just before the New South Wales border. My black lace-ups were already starting to look dust-worn. When I kicked them in the red gravel outside the Moree truck stop café, small crimson grains settled into the holes, sifting into my white socks, leaving spots that looked like blood, as though tiny shoe insects had bumbled in, biting in procession.

After Armidale, my first ride had dropped me at the truck stop and given me twenty bucks for some food. I said, 'It's fine, don't.' That guy had toddler seats in the back of the car and played Classic FM from Brisbane. In a charity shop in Newcastle, I'd found a flick knife, a strangely beautiful thing. Gold, carved, with a small clip. Five dollars. I bought it because it made me feel tough and because, along with the small bottle of amyl nitrate, I thought it might come in handy. I had no idea how to use it. None. But I kept my hand on it all the way to Moree, while the guy with the toddler seat explained the music of Bartok to me and quoted things his toddlers said. At the end of each story of toddler cuteness, he trailed off into a slow chuckle, shaking his head in wonder. I waited for the turn, for the mask to come off, waited for the moment when I would realise his true wickedness, but it did not come. When he dropped me at the truck stop, he told me to be careful, to watch out for myself.

After the toddler-seat man drove off, tooting his horn cheerfully, I tried to order yoghurt in the truck stop and the blonde woman said, 'We don't serve health freaks here.' I bought a bag of peanuts and licked the salt from the foil packet.

Hairy Guy was outside, holding the door of his ute open. My deal with myself was this: whenever I could, I'd get rides from cafés or truck stops. And I'd write down the number plate and tell someone – the waitress in the café, a guy in another truck, anyone – where I was going. That, I thought, that would keep me safe. But anyway, nothing I'd done had kept me safe, not the right things or the wrong things. Danger followed me, and perhaps I deserved it. Some girls, when they are hurt, eat an entire town, watching their bodies swell like a fortress. I had done this, eating until I was numb and wide. Some girls, when they are wounded, vomit up the town they ate, and I had done this too, feeling the burning in my throat, hoarse like a scream. Some girls batter their bodies with drugs or, like me, with danger.

But Kerouac and his boys jumped in and out of cars. They stuck their thumbs out on the highway and they were free, and I would be free too. The driver of the ute rested his hand on the upper frame of the cab door—prominent knuckles, neatly trimmed square fingernails. Clean, too. My own nails were already caked with dirt that I couldn't get rid of, no matter how many times I scraped a bobby pin beneath them. Khaki canvas fluttered across the ute trailer; a swag poked out. There was no dog and no sign of another ride.

Let me be clear here: I had no deadline, no outcome, no one waiting. There was no one to care for me, only myself, and I had never learned the lessons of caring. There was only me and my backpack full of books and my black lace-ups and a desperate need to get away. I'd already disappeared, though, and the more buried I was, the better. The more buried I was, the deeper in the earth, the more chance I had of being new, of making a new me, a new story. That was my plan, as much as I had. I got into the ute and hoped that it would get me further away from where I was.

Hairy Guy had a name – Paul – and he could take me north, as far as Emerald. It was closer to the end of the country, closer to the land's boundary. And so I went with him. I told him I'd come from Melbourne, where I was studying law – I'd always fancied studying law – and I was taking a break between courses. I knew less about Melbourne than I did about law, but he didn't ask me about the city. He just said I must be smart if I was going to be a lawyer and was it just for the money, and I said no, I wanted to be a lawyer so that I could help people.

He said, 'Help crims, you mean? Help them get off?'

I watched the cotton fields flash past outside the window. 'No. Help the others. Not the crims. Help innocent people.'

'Victims?'

I shrugged.

He said, 'How would you know? How would you know who's the victim and who's guilty?'

I said, 'I guess that's why I'm studying law. To find out.'

'To find out how to tell who's lying and who's telling the truth? Double-crossing people, you mean?'

'Double-crossing?'

'When you come down and ask the crim all the questions and then another lawyer asks him again.'

'Cross-examining?'

'Yeah. That. Will you do that? Is that what lawyers do?'

My pulse battered at the base of my throat, but I nodded. 'That's right.'

We camped overnight somewhere in the desert. We'd gone so far north that the land and sky had already opened up. We ate soft cheese and white bread and he lit a fire and hung an actual billy on it. Yes, I thought. I am far away now. I am on the road and the world will never find me and I will become someone else. What happens will happen whether I will it to or not. I don't know what I thought I would find. Flames cut across the night, embers sparking. Hairy Guy – Paul – was a shadowy shape on the other side of the flames, his beard looking one second red, the other black. I'd untied my enamel mug, purchased in the army surplus store in Sydney, and poured the billy tea in. It was as thick as the black above me.

We slept by the fire, me in my sleeping bag, him out of his swag, and all night he shuffled closer and closer to me, while I shuffled away from him inch by inch until I woke with the smell of smoke, where the end of my sleeping bag had melted into the embers of the fire.

The next day he dropped me at another truck stop, and held my hand for a minute too long, and then I stepped out of the ute and stood on the highway in the sweltering sun, waiting for my next ride, waiting for something hopeful, waiting for something to change.

THERE WAS NO YOGHURT in any of the truck stops, only burgers and bad coffee and a feeling that I didn't know this country, my country. The further north I went, the more alien the country and the people became. On the outer boundary of Emerald, I camped on my own beneath a tree by a creek bed and was woken in the morning by a cluster of locals speaking their language. At first, when I woke in my half-burned sleeping bag, the words seemed to be birdsong blending in with the song of the river. I lay there, trying to separate out the sounds, trying to decipher the music, while I blinked myself awake. In the night, the temperature had dropped down low, and I'd layered myself in socks and leggings. When the sun came up, I felt that I was being roasted and grilled, basted by the melody of the language washing over me. I wriggled out of my sleeping bag and headed down to the creek barefoot to rinse the grain from my face. Sand clumped beneath my toes, and when I set one foot into the water, the sweet cool of it stilled me.

Behind me, the talk escalated into shouts and catcalls, a cacophony that frightened me with its strangeness. Someone was shouting behind me, something urgent in the tone. I knew the sounds of escalating violence, had grown up attuned to the swift changes in mood that might turn to a punch, a hit. This talk lacked that undercurrent, but still my toes trembled a little in the cool dark water. I wanted to feel at home here; I wanted these words, these accents, to feel familiar to me. I wanted to feel a part of it. But I didn't, and when the hand grabbed at my wrist I jumped, letting out a little shriek.

The woman's pink nails dug into the skin of my forearm. She said, 'There's crocs in there, honey. Just 'cause you can't see 'em doesn't mean they're not there.' She jerked me back, away from the shoreline, then kept her hand on my wrist, her gaze on the far side of the river. She held her other hand up, instructing me to wait, to listen, to watch. Cicadas burned somewhere deep in the bush, and the swell of heat accompanied the undulating tide of noise: a chirruping, the soft and quiet swirl of water, and, somewhere nearby, the ck-ck-ck of an unfamiliar bird. Sweat pooled under my breasts, the sun making my limbs soft. On the far side of the river, one of the long grey logs twisted suddenly, its jaws clicking open before it slid, rocket-fast, into the water.

The woman lifted her hand from my forearm then, her face splitting in a grin. Nodding to my pack and sleeping bag beneath the tree, a few feet from the river, she said, 'You sleep here last night?'

I nodded, thinking of that moving grey croc, a sick swell in my stomach.

She nodded at the water, heaving with crocodiles. 'You bloody lucky, mate. These buggers just waiting like that.'

She called something in her language to the rest of the group, their combined laughter mixing with the bush birds while I felt the sickness in my stomach rise like yeast. I had not yet read *Candide*, but I'd absorbed, somehow, the belief that naivety would protect me, despite the evidence.

They waved me off, all of them, as I shouldered my pack and scuttled back to the road. Unwashed, teeth uncleaned, and with the woman's words ringing after me. I was lucky. Bloody lucky.

I walked in the heat to the highway and waited until a couple picked me up. Her with grey short hair, a clay pendant at her neck; him, hands on his lap in the passenger seat, holding a map up and reciting distances as though it were a competition. They asked me nothing, and I volunteered nothing, and when they dropped me at the Longreach truck stop I was surprised that she got out of the car and hugged me.

In the trucker's café the waitress waited, clicking her pen against a cork clipboard, her pink uniform slightly stained under the armpits, while I scanned the menu. 'Vegetarian?' she repeated, when I told her. 'You could have an egg, I suppose. Or chicken?'

I had an egg, and I squirted the yolk down the front of my top. I'd packed three singlet tops into my pack, carefully rolled, the way I'd been told to do, everything tucked inside everything else. In Sydney, Sylvie had said, 'Take three of everything: pants, bra, T-shirt. You can wash in between.'

I scratched the egg yolk off the counter, and then used the end of a teaspoon to scrape the dried yolk from my fingernail. Paid, counting out coins, trying to keep the precious notes in my wallet. The restrooms were outside, a small brick building with a picture of a ram for men and a hornless ewe for the women. The signs said *Rams* and *Ewes*. Although I had neither horns nor wool, I went into the Ewes and stripped off my singlet top, scrubbing at it in the cold bore water from the tap, holding my nose at the sulphuric smell. There was no soap in the Ewes, so I squeezed a dab of shampoo on it. Bubbles foamed up in the sink, soaking the whole top. I wrung it out, dripping suds and water onto the stones beneath my feet, and let the wet cotton cool me.

Heat whirred outside, so thick I could almost see the particles twirling, melting together. Sunlight bounced off the glass doors of the truck stop, making diamonds against the words curved over the top of the window, scribbled in thick paint: *Burgers! Chops! $5 Monday special breakfast! Truckers discount!*

. . .

Fury

Toddy emerged from the glass doors like a hero, like a sign. Bandy legs, a round gut curving softly over King Gee shorts, sun glinting off the dome of his head. He clocked me standing by the petrol pump, my pack at my feet, water dripping off my shirt, my stolen Ray-Bans on the top of my head.

Truckers back then tended to look tough: tattoos, thickened skin from the sun, broad backs and bellies from sitting up there in the cabin for days on end, darting eyes from the lack of sleep and, sometimes, the ephedrine they took to keep them driving impossible distances in impossible times. Toddy had the curving gut, but his eyes lacked the darting, desperate quality, and I could see only one tattoo: Earth, its oceans shaded in green, the land mapped in dark grey. Later, I asked him about it: why the globe? He grinned into the windscreen, said, 'It reminds me that the whole world matters. Not just me.'

Already, my brief flash of blindness had started to open me up, to give me a kind of second sight. That's what I told myself. Across the forecourt, I singled Toddy out. Like a battered dog in the shelter waiting for the human with a soft touch, I waited till I saw that round-bellied truck driver, and then I chose him. We walked towards each other at the same time – me with my hand above my eyes, him squinting directly into the sun.

We spoke at the same time.

Me: 'Where are you headed?'

Him: 'It's dangerous to hitchhike.'

I flashed to that earlier night, a school night, the two boys whooping as we lifted off the tarmac, the bruises that stayed on my skin for weeks after I'd rolled from the car. But this was different. It had to be different.

I had to be different.

I said, 'I know. That's why I'm not hitchhiking. I'm asking you for a lift. And if you say yes, I'm going to that phone box over there and I'll phone my friend in Darwin and tell her your number plate and where you're going to drop me and what time I'm getting in the truck. If I don't arrive, she'll call the police and give them your number plate. If that's not okay, I can wait for another truck.'

I thought I was so smart, so smooth.

When Toddy laughed, his mouth opened wide and I could see the gaps at the back where his teeth had come out. He said, 'Better go call your friend.'

In the phone box, I watched the silver dial turn, listened to the empty purr of the dial tone. I moved my mouth and nodded my head. When I climbed up into the cabin of the truck, Toddy said, 'Okay?'

'Yep. My friend's taken your number down, so watch yourself.'

He did that big open-mouthed laugh again.

When he asked me about my friend later, I thought about all those pretty girls, the ones who had me as second-in-command; I thought of Penny and the party and I thought of Sylvie and her long, tanned legs and I said, 'She's just a better version of me. Prettier. Funnier. Better.' I'd trained myself to say it, to get in with the put-downs before anyone else did.

I realise now that when I said 'better' what I meant was 'skinnier'. I was not a skinny girl, and when I tried to eat less, to be thinner, I became consumed with the desire to fill myself with food, to make myself wider, stronger, thicker. My value as a girl lay in taking up less space; I understood this and I longed to be desired, to demonstrate that I had the value required. So, in high school, I fasted for days at a time, drinking endless cups of coffee to keep my appetite at bay. Afterwards, I ate and ate and ate, filling myself until my skin stretched, and my rage was buried beneath layers of fat. The truth was that, like so many girls, I needed to demand more room, not less; but I was not yet brave enough to know it.

IT TOOK TWO DAYS to drive across the border to the Northern Territory, across the wide stretch of the desert with its stars sharp in the unlit sky. The cabin had two sections. When Toddy climbed into the main section to rest, he closed the curtain so I could sleep in the neat bunk behind it. I slept while he drove, then I woke, stretching in the curtained cabin and climbing over the front seat to sit beside him. He asked me about my life, and I told him pretty much the whole truth, or as much of it as I could own. It was the first time, the only time, that I'd spoken it all in a series of sentences. The only time, the first time, that I'd not made up a name, a family, a more exotic version. There seemed no point, stuck in the confined cabin with the scrub spread out in front of the windscreen, as low and long as an ocean.

He insisted on buying my dinner in the truck stops, making excuses about truckers' discounts and how it was easier that way. 'You're keeping me entertained,' he said, and then turned off the road, drew the curtain across and slept. Some time in the night, while he was snoring, I climbed out of the cab, stepped down to the ground and stood in my bare feet. The ground was icy beneath me, the dirt forming small crystals that caught between my toes. Earth seemed to flow beneath my feet; I felt that I could hear with my soles, with my toes, with the pores of my skin, felt that the very ground was pulsing in a way that ground did not pulse in the city.

I'd never seen such darkness. The sky was thick with stars, but the black between them was dense, more like earth than sky. I wandered away from the square shape of the truck. Warning images flashed up briefly; scenes from films and books, paintings with lost girls in the bush, stories of wanderers dead and dying because of the brutality of the outback.

But this did not feel brutal.

Growing up, we owned nothing, no land, no house, and we moved from place to place at the whim of landlords. I felt myself to be connected by a whisper-thin thread to any place we lived in, to any story, though I searched through the pages of every book hoping to find someone like me, a story like mine.

Sometimes, though rarely, we would have an outing. A daytrip. We would drive somewhere: a chocolate factory; a mini-castle built in the fifties by a lovelorn husband; a garden shop. There was no wilderness. Nature was carefully contained and curated. It was the best my mother could do: an instructed leisure, facilitated through cars and highways and *Women's Weekly* magazines. Gift shops and visitor centres.

Here, I could see no margins, no curation. I walked until I felt the darkness envelop me, until the stars and the earth merged, so that I could barely tell if I was standing on earth or sky. Arms outstretched, I twirled, and it seemed as though the stars washed over me, over my hands and face and feet. Stars seemed to echo on the earth, bright on my feet, as though I were burning in the galaxy among them, and I felt the pulsing of the earth and the strange song of the sky and something swelled in me, something alien. A kind of peace is what it was, a fluttering of happiness and of hope, so unfamiliar as to be unrecognisable.

The windscreen of the Kenwood was wide and clear, and through it I watched the bush turn to desert, and the desert sky turn to an ocean of thick black, dotted with blade-sharp stars.

Somewhere between Threeways and Katherine, Toddy asked me if I wanted to drive. 'No,' I squealed, 'I can't drive.' God, the terror of it.

'Here,' he said, 'move the gears.'

He tooted the mournful horn while I did, and I laughed like him, open-mouthed, head thrown back.

We talked and talked and talked. Decades later, when the BBC asked me to write a short story, I wrote one about a kind truck driver who missed his mother and unexpectedly found love with a waitress in a truck stop. I'd forgotten about Toddy; I only now realise that it was him in that story, and that I wanted to give him a love story. I wanted to give him something, anything.

It was just before Katherine that we started fighting.

He'd never had kids. Always wanted them, he said. Would have been proud of a kid like me, with my brains.

'How do you know I'm brainy?'

He tooted the slow moan of the trucker's horn. 'Listen to you, you never shut up. Going on with your big ideas. You're making my brain hurt.'

I smacked him on the arm, and he added, 'But in a good way.' His hands clenched the wheel. 'Yep. I'd be proud if you were my kid. But I wouldn't let you go off into the who-knows-where on your own. Not without a bloke beside you.'

I said, 'Oh, for God's sake, Toddy. Like a bloke is going to protect me. It's blokes who are the bloody danger. Where have you been living, honestly?'

He shook his head again. 'You just shouldn't be out there on the road. I don't like dropping you out here, middle of nowhere.'

'It's not up to you.' And then, although it was patently untrue, I added, 'I can take care of myself.'

'You're just a girl.'

'I'm as strong as anyone. You're being stupid.'

Somehow, we were shouting, swearing, slamming fists on the dashboard. Anger bubbled just beneath my skin, waiting for someone to call it up.

'I'm an adult. A woman.' Then I said, 'Jesus. You're not my father.' Ridiculous, how easy it was to become an obstreperous teenager.

Toddy's mouth bent into a crooked shape. 'I never said I was.'

We drove the rest of the way in a strained silence. I'd calculated that I had enough money for a night or two at the Katherine youth hostel, so Toddy drove right to the door, the long road train curving behind him. He stopped outside the ramshackle building, right by the sign that said *YHA*.

'Okay?' His voice was small.

I grabbed my pack from the cabin. 'Yep. Thanks for the ride.' I kept my eyes on my feet while the truck drove away, tooting once more that mournful song.

The hostel was almost full: Danish backpackers, mainly, and one or two Americans. I unfolded my sleeping sheet in the dorm room and lay on it, staring at the ceiling. Dust floated down from the slow fan chk-chking above me. A gecko scratched its way up the wall. Time did what it does, and I waited for something to happen, too tired to move. Eventually, I grabbed a tin of beans and the single pan from the bottom of my pack. In the kitchen, one of the Danish backpackers tossed garlic, herbs and something meaty in a pan, her wrist turning with the ease of a well-weighted hula hoop. She smiled at me with my one tin of baked beans, my enamel bowl. She poured tomatoes into the pan. 'I'm Eva. Are you Kacey?'

Startled, I nodded, then looked up at the slatted air vents, half-expecting spies to emerge. The fat barrister, maybe, with his wig askew, pointing at me, delighted with further evidence of my wickedness. Hitchhiking, shouting at random strangers etc.

Eva nodded towards the door marked *Reception: Office Hours ONLY*. 'There's a message for you.'

I knocked on the reception door. I had no idea of the time, nor of the office hours. A man in a stained singlet and torn grey shorts opened the door. Grey hair poked out around the top and sleeves of his singlet, curling against the leather of his skin. The grey of his beard was tinged with yellow, as were his teeth. 'You Kacey?'

I nodded and he handed me a torn piece of notepaper. On it, the words:

Teddy (??) called. Said sorry. Also your friend is not better than you and also you can take care of yourself but make sure you do and please be safe.

Red squiggles surrounded the words and the last three – *please be safe* – were underlined three times. The man leaning against the door said, 'He made me read it back to him twice before he'd hang up.'

I folded the note three times for luck, and slipped it into the bottom of my backpack, inside the first page of the F. Scott Fitzgerald stories, *The Price Was High*.

I DON'T REMEMBER much of the party. Another party, a different party. This one was in a narrow terrace house, lit with bare bulbs painted with swirls of colour, and we drank riesling from casks, the foil bladders torn from the cardboard boxes and dotted about the kitchen like balloons. There was a wooden table, unpolished, unpainted, wedged against the back door; dinner plates with cabanossi and chunks of cheese covered the table, along with paper cups and ashtrays improvised from coffee mugs and saucers. Most people there wore Dr Martens, the black boots that went halfway up the shin, and the music was Billy Bragg and Bronski Beat. 'A New England' blasted out on repeat for what seemed like hours, while we danced and mimed on the tottery stairs.

I did not wear DMs. I wore a dark green linen dress I'd found in a charity shop, a remnant from the 1950s with endless pleats that twirled out when I danced. Black cotton shoes, made in China, and I couldn't remember what I was supposed to think or feel about China with these people, my new friends. We'd met on a street corner. He was selling *Resistance*, the badly printed, badly worded newspaper of the Young Socialists. The paper was flimsy; he had it folded across his arm, and a young woman with a perfectly shorn head handed him a new paper whenever he sold one. Which was infrequently. On the far side of the mall, there was another group of them.

The collar of my school blouse had an ink stain on it – I seemed always to be carrying broken pens, seemed always to be splattering ink on my fingers or clothes or papers. He said something witty about the ink, and about the school uniform, and asked me what I thought about Russia, what I thought about Palestine.

He wore combat trousers from an army surplus store and a hessian bag over his hip. When he asked me about Palestine, he leaned down to hear me better, the darks of his eyes almost blending with the brown irises. Brown moppish hair and a slightly crooked smile. The young woman listened too, and we sat on a bench and kept talking until the other group had stopped selling their papers and joined us. Everyone was equal, everyone deserved power: that was the message of the flimsy newspaper, and that was the message of the combat-trousers-wearing man, and he listened to me, leaning closer and closer, listening to the words that I spoke about a country I knew barely anything about.

The party happened some weeks after that. I'd dragged Sylvie to a Young Socialists meeting at which ten or so people sat in a back room of a different terrace and drank instant coffee and talked about the possibilities of revolution in our coastal industrial town. Sylvie crossed her long legs and refused the instant coffee but later said she thought that one socialist, the one with the combat trousers and the brown eyes and the crooked smile, he was all right. Fanciable. David. David Fox. I think we might have sung 'Fox on the Run' while pretending to be him, David Fox, loping around the mall.

My mother had married her small, broken man two years earlier. After they married, I stayed with them briefly in the shack he lived in and then with one of my sisters. Then, when it was clear there wasn't another home for me, I moved to a hostel in the centre of the city, measuring out meals and eking out coins for the laundry. Over lunch at school, when friends complained about their parents, I laughed along, as though there were someone watching me in the evenings, checking on my progress. David Fox and the shorn-headed girl and their small gang, they did not ask me about my parents or about curfew times.

In the grimy terrace house while Billy Bragg played, I drank paper cup after paper cup of the riesling, and then moved on to cups of fizzy red soft drink diluted with vodka, and then, when I couldn't walk and could barely talk, David Fox offered to take me back to the hostel. There's a memory of being tucked into his car, someone clicking a seatbelt across my lap while I laughed; and then of my head outside the car, the breeze like water on my face. When David Fox opened the door outside the hostel I fell out onto the grass and lay there laughing up at the changing sky, stunned by the way the trees moved and swayed against the upside down of the world, and by the way the grass beneath me kept turning, turning. And then crawling to the flowerbed to vomit, trying to hold my perfectly pleated dress away from the dirt, away from the sick.

My legs kept buckling beneath me, so David Fox carried me to my room. Water. There was that. Without the beautiful air, the sky circling above me, I thought I would suffocate like a fish from lack of water. He must have got a glass for me, because when I woke up in the morning there was a full glass of water on my desk, right next to my balled-up knickers. I was still wearing my bra, but it was undone at the back, flapping against my breasts. I swatted away the strangeness of this, the discomfort of it. Later, when Sylvie began her short-lived romance with David Fox, something troubled me, something scraped at my nerves, but I couldn't name it. I wondered if it was jealousy. I was often jealous of Sylvie.

Fury

David Fox didn't mention the water or the knickers, not until long after the party. Not until after I had made the pre-dawn trip to Sydney with Sylvie, for her to wash out his unwelcome seed. I'd stopped going to meetings by then, bored with the posturing and pretending, the plotting for a revolution that would never happen, the talk of equality that was entirely theoretical. Stopped going to their parties or selling their flimsy paper. But he didn't stop.

The Hunter Street mall was the place to buy books, games, clothes. The place to drink coffee. To wander up and down, hoping that something might happen. I was in my school uniform again, in the last months of school, waiting for my life to begin. I'd come out of the second-hand bookshop, holding bags of books in my arms, and there he was.

We stood awkwardly on the corner of the mall, making polite chitchat, and I avoided mentioning my doubts about the likelihood of actual revolution. Eventually, I said, 'My boyfriend is waiting for me, so – um – nice to run into you, David.'

His face flattened, as though hit by something wet. 'You've got a boyfriend? Since when?'

'Since about six months ago, I guess.' I thought about his posturing with Sylvie, thought about me and Sylvie chanting, *It's different for a man,* and I added, 'He's kind.' I did not add, although I knew it to be true, *He's gay*.

He grabbed my hand. 'Kacey, since that night we made love, I haven't stopped thinking about you.'

The words were so hammy that I honestly assumed he was making some kind of joke, doing a performance riff on movie parting scenes, and so I laughed. I expected him to mime violins, or swooning. Instead, his face did the strange flattening again, his head jerking back, turtle-like, on his neck. 'I mean it.'

My throat began to tighten. 'Sorry, what? The night we what?'

His hand was enormous, his skin papery.

'It meant a lot to me.'

One of the paper bags broke as I clutched the books closer to my chest. I bent to gather them up, piling them into my school backpack. There were three Jane Austens, the *Collected Works of T.S. Eliot*, a pile of study guides, some assorted new novels. There were no fairytales, with their coded warnings of wolves and woodcutters. I was not yet old enough for those. The tiny shred of anger was so small I could barely feel it, could barely notice its path. Instead I smiled, backing away, books raised to my chest like armour.

'Stay in touch,' he said.

And I smiled and bobbed my head, almost a curtsy, and said, 'Sure. Take care, David.'

I said nothing else, not a word. I held my tongue so hard I almost drew blood.

THE HANDS ON THE WHEEL beside me were so pale that they were almost the colour of ash. Veins pulsed slowly in his wrist, below the black leather strap of his watch. It was gold, the watch, possibly a cheap gold, possibly tinted aluminium: I couldn't tell. This is the time in my life when I can't tell the difference between real and fake, true and false. Below the wristband, a bone jutted out, a small scab rubbed raw by the leather. Perhaps the leather was fake too. His shirt had cuffs that folded back beyond the wrist, a detail that seemed impressive to me, or at the very least notable, when he picked me up outside of Humpty Doo, where I'd spent the night camping alone down the back of the pub.

I didn't have a tent. I'd strapped my sleeping bag – now melted – to the outside of my pack, along with the enamel cup that I thought made me a real wanderer. But I had no voice, barely a whisper, no compass, no trust fund and, frankly, no clue. I'd slept on a foam bedroll I'd bought in Armidale, swiping mosquitoes and then, after the heat dropped away in the pre-dawn hours, shivering so hard my bones hurt.

All night I could hear the drinkers at the Humpty Doo pub, the laughter and shouting washing over me like the ocean. In the morning, I found my hairbrush at the bottom of my pack, cleaned my teeth and washed my face in the public toilets behind the pub, then slathered sweet-smelling moisturiser – jasmine-scented, the smell of a Sydney spring – all over my face and hands. And then I stood on the road in front of the pub and waited.

Humpty Doo pub was on a main road, the road that led straight to the Top End. I stood by the roadside, pack on my back and hand down at my side, all casual, just lifting my hand when a car drove by, like I didn't really mind one way or another. By 11 a.m., I really did mind, not just one way, but every way. When a dark Mercedes drove past me, I screamed every word I knew at it, and then I made some up. It was their *responsibility* to rescue me, idiots. A kombi drove past, too, with two girls in the front next to a bearded driver. The girls turned their faces to stare at me, a flash of open-mouthed blondeness as they hooted past. Dust pleated up behind them and sprinkled onto my lace-ups, settling with the humiliating tease of that jaunty toot-toot-toot. They were the right kind of girls. Even in the flash of a drive-by I could see it: bikini tops, tans, long blonde and effortless.

Heat baked down on me, shifting from the caress of warmth that had made me soften in the centre. Here, outside the Humpty Doo pub, with dust settling on my arms and legs, the heat was harder: smashing into my face, thickening in my throat. All I wanted was to swim, to dive into the ocean and feel myself swallowed up. Thumb pointed nonchalantly towards the road, I swayed, imagining diving into the bliss of blue. But there was just dust, and heat, and the roar of another engine down the track.

The station wagon was blue, the kind of blue that would have been called powder-blue when I was a kid. I remember longing desperately for a powder-blue bedspread. Powder-blue seemed sophisticated, subtle. And I guess I wanted to be subtle. Or, at least, I knew enough to know that I wasn't.

He leaned over to wind the window down, the bone on his wrist clunking against the glass. Gold-rimmed glasses perched on his nose. He wore a collared shirt – it was the first time I'd seen a collar in the ten days it had taken me to get this far. Truck drivers and roo hunters don't have much use for a neat button-down.

I'd already slid into the front seat before I could assess his face. Anyway, how would I assess it? How do you decide if the face of the man driving the car alone, the face of the man offering you a lift, is the face of a rapist or a murderer? He wore a silver stud in one ear, he had classical music playing and his name was Michael.

I'd kept my flick knife in the money belt at my waist. The belt had twenty dollars in it, and that knife; I kept the pouch on my left-hand side, so that I could get to the knife if I needed to.

I wasn't strong. At a free community yoga class earlier that year, I'd been the only person who couldn't use her own arms to lower herself to a lying pose. I'd flopped, fish-like, my face bouncing slightly on the floorboards. And I wasn't fit. I'd spent the best part of a year smoking dope every day, drinking every night, eating bags of salted crisps while I tried to forget about the preceding night. And in that year I had not run, not once, anywhere. I had not skipped, or skated, or swum. I had waited, wasted. And I was not brave. Everything made me frightened: the darkness of a river, the bare sky at night, the hum of a city. I had no sense of my own safety, no sense of my own care. But if I had to, I would take that knife from my money belt, and I would slash that ear-ringed motherfucker across his throat, because I knew what happened when you tried to call a man out for what he'd done to you, and I knew precisely how much the world cared.

'Have you come from the pub?' He leaned forward to turn the music down. His wedding ring glinted in the sun. Silver, a thin band. Unusual.

'Nope.' I stared out the window, trying to decide where I might be from this time, trying to decide on a name, a story.

Anything, anyone, was better than my own true one, which had nothing in it of value, nothing of worth. I plummed my vowels up a bit, rounding out my words. 'I'm visiting. From Kent.'

'Kent, England?'

'That's right.' I'd met a girl from Kent in a café in Sydney. She had blonde hair, dimples, wore fluoro midriff tops that showed off her cute belly. Her accent was bouncy, like her. Easy to study, easy to mimic.

'Whereabouts in Kent?'

I had no idea where Kerri was from. The knife was hot against my palm. Before Longreach, I'd told a ride I was from Denmark and he said he'd travelled there as a boy. Thank Christ he spoke no Danish. After that, I'd decided to keep it English-speaking. I knew of one place in Kent, thanks to Chaucer and Miss Pitt, an ambitious English teacher. 'Canterbury.'

'Right. Always wanted to go there. England, I mean. I've never been. What's it like?'

I thought of the books I'd devoured as a child. I thought of Maisie and the naughty twins, and I thought of the girl from the bush and her mettle. 'Green. Really very green.' I kept my words round, tried to hold it all in, the way Kerri did. Gahden. Mah-vellous.

Michael raised his eyebrows. I couldn't tell if he was buying it or not, so I switched tack. 'And you? You're from . . . ?' I let it slide away like that. As though I were at a dinner with multiple forks, not sitting in my own sweat, dust lining the inside of my knees, on a track from Humpty Doo.

He asked me why I was in Australia, what on earth had brought me here. And all alone. He looked sideways at me when he said that, alone, and his hand slid off the steering wheel onto the gear stick between us. I angled my knees away from him, turning to the window, watching the red and brown land rush past, and I ran my fingers along the carved metal of my knife.

I kept my hand on my knife and kept my lips moving, my mouth talking, all the way to Darwin. I told Michael the story of how my father – a medic from London – had left my mother and me when I was a kid. Five, I decided. Not even in primary school. Siblings? None, definitely none. And my mother?

I was about to say that she was dead – I liked the idea of the travelling orphan – but then I thought about where I was. Driving through the middle of nowhere, with no trucks or cars in sight, with a stranger. I said that my mother had decided to visit Australia too, and was waiting for me in Darwin. Even as I said it, I was aware that the edges of my story didn't quite connect, but I was in too deep. I added, 'I was supposed to pay for her to come out. Since my father . . .' I trailed off. 'Left.'

The pale light of the ocean started to come into view and Michael slowed the station wagon a little. He said, 'Do you want to earn some extra money while you're here?'

I did. That was what I was here for, after all.

He gave me that sideways look again. 'There are quite a lot of ways a girl can make extra cash.'

He looked back to the road, shifted into cruise control. My mouth ran dry.

Michael pointed to the water. 'You go out on the boats as a cook, you'll make thousands.' He tapped his finger on the wheel in time to the song from the pasta advertisement. 'They're always looking for girls to cook. I'll drive by the docks, if you like, so you can see where to go. You just turn up. They're always after girls.'

Just the phrase made me shiver. I didn't notice the end point: *they're always after girls*. I only heard two words: *the docks*.

The first time I ran away, I ran to the docks. No, it wasn't the first time, of course. I ran away daily, taking my clothes in plastic bags, knocking on Aunty June's door, begging to be allowed to live with her family. They had no room for a little girl, they said, each time giving me an Iced Vo-Vo before they took me home. For years I believed that Aunty June was my real aunt, my blood relative, that I belonged in her family – or that I belonged in some other family, anyway. Don't all children believe this, or hope for it?

The first time I ran away properly, that was to the docks. I was five. My brother was eight. Perhaps my brother intended us to go for the day, but I believed – hoped – that we were going forever. He held my hand on the bus. The docks were forty minutes away on the bus, and what they had there were ships from other countries. Ships with flags on them. Ships that would go far away, take me far away. It was easy to prise my hand from my brother's, easy. And I was little, small enough to dodge him, running between the legs of the workers unloading boxes, small enough to bolt up the long ladder of a ship with a Japanese flag flying above it. Small enough, surely, to be put into the pocket of one of the sailors and taken home with them, to be their girl?

This is what I remember: the laughing sailors holding me up above the decking, while the frenzy of the docks buzzed below. This: held aloft by those laughing sailors, like a trophy, a prize, while my brother shouted for me. I could see him, small below me, and I wanted him to cry, to collapse on the ground sobbing for me, wailing the way I so often wailed. But he would not wail. He stood firm. Even from up there, I could see him thinking, making a plan, being brave. He was brave, that boy, even when my father roared at him, lifted him, tossed him like a bag of chaff. My brother would tremble, but he would not break, not then. And so I relented, shouting down to him, shouting to the sailors that the boy down there, that was my brother. They gave us sweet rice with a sticky sauce and promised that I could go live with them when I was a bigger girl.

Running away started then, and it always made things better. Running away always worked.

Blue rose up flat like a painting, so upright that I thought we might smack into it. 'The docks,' I said. 'Yes, take me there.'

He slipped his hand from the steering wheel, dropped it onto my leg. 'There are other ways. To make cash. Easier.' When he grinned this time, I could see the black of his fillings. One long finger slipped into the fold between my legs, tracing the ragged fringe of the cut-off jeans. His finger rested there, as though separate from him, a being with its own will. I grappled with the antique clasp of the beautiful carved flick knife inside my money belt. I would cut his hand off if he tried, I'd cut his face, slash his tyres; I wasn't going there again.

Flat-roofed buildings flashed by outside the car, strange desert fruit. For the first time, I noticed the redness of his face, the man beside me, the man with his finger sliding between my thighs. The safety catch on the knife was disconcertingly secure and the man beside me – how hard would it be, I wondered, for him to wrestle it from me? All my bluster, my bravado, but I couldn't be Dean Moriarty, I couldn't be Odysseus or Quixote, not any of the boys, because any of them, those man-heroes with their own knives, they would overpower me the way I'd been overpowered before.

I took my hand out of the pouch and pointed my knees towards the window. I made myself small, as small as I felt. Signs began to appear for the town centre, for lodges, for sites of interest.

'Actually, drop me here,' I said. 'Please.'

He didn't reply, so I added, 'My friends will be waiting.'

I'd lost track of the lies I'd told by now. Was I the English girl waiting for her mother? Or the adventurer from another city, looking for work? He didn't say a word, just slid to the side of the road and waited while I got my pack from the back seat. I didn't thank him for the ride, and I didn't wave him off cheerily. Dirt clumped around the wheels as he drove away, while I turned to the horizon. Tilting at windmills, my useless lance in my pocket, my trusty pack on my back.

HEAT BEAT UP from the grass outside Lameroo Lodge, great billowing puffs of it like dust from a rug. Under the gum trees, backpackers newly arrived in Darwin lolled like kangaroos, their limbs stretched and crooked, making little noises as they shifted and turned in the shimmering haze. Sometimes a cackle, a caw, from a cluster at the far end of the grass, and later, some soft murmuring. People had coupled, or grouped, had made themselves into packs and tribes.

At one of the truck stops on the way to the Top End, I'd walked the perimeter of the fence. Wire stretched as far as I could see; when I tucked my hand into it, I thought of the girl in *Picnic at Hanging Rock*, the one in love with Miranda, the one who is on the outskirts, who is lost, who is alone. When I read that book, I knew who I was supposed to identify with, and yet it was that lost and lonely one who felt so kindred to me. And there, at that fence somewhere near Kackadilla or some such place, my fingers looped through the wire and I held my face against it, longing, lonely, but desperate to be alone, desperate to be silent. An emu walked on the other side of the fence, its legs bending into triangles, its neck stretching along the ground, its beak a sword. We watched each other, each of us alone and ancient. Now, outside the lodge, I was that emu, walking the perimeter, staring in at the clusters of people grouped and huddled on the grass. How did they do that, form themselves like that? I wanted to be with them. I did not want to be with them. I wanted to be indifferent.

Lameroo Lodge was the hostel where all travellers to this north end of Australia ended up eventually. Inside, my eyes blinking in the darkened hallway, I counted out my dollars. I had enough for a room for two nights. I paid in advance and spent almost an hour in the shower, watching the dirt run off my body. Red water pooled at my feet, smearing across the chipped green and yellow tiles. Someone hammered on the door, shouting at me to hurry up, but I kept letting the water wash over me, opening my mouth so it could pour in. I'd been so parched for so long. I washed my clothes and put them in the industrial dryer, and I sat on a spindly chair, reading one of the fat novels that someone had left on the 'Take, Leave' table. I left a Carlos Castaneda that I'd picked up in Katherine and, although I'd already read it, I took *Of Human Bondage*. Feet up on the table, I read and let the churning of the dryer lull me to a kind of peace. Pacified by the warmth and the rhythm and the slowness of Maugham's words, my head dropped to my chest; I kept thinking about my father, his chin drooping while he harrumphed, 'I'm not asleep.' I thought about that and I laughed, and when I lifted my head someone was there, watching me.

He was golden. No, moonlight white. White hair, pale skin, grey eyes. He was laughing too, and for a moment I thought that perhaps I could be the girl, the one in the film, the one who has the nice things, the pretty things. So, I smiled at him and lifted my knees for him to pass, and I wanted to be able to play the flirting game, but I had no idea how, none.

He had a pillowcase full, I guessed, of washing. The pillowcase had a picture of Santa painted on it with Hobbytex, as though his mother or aunt had painted it carefully from a stencil, proud of her craft skills.

He took his shirt off and put it in the machine with the contents of the Hobbytex pillowcase, and I watched him, the folds in his pale skin as he bent. When he straightened up, he smiled again then nodded at the pile of books, said, 'Are these yours? Mind if I take the Castaneda? I love him. He's a genius.'

'Is he? They seem like trash to me.' It was too late to snap the words back, too late to stop that thing I always did, needing to be better, smarter, louder than the boys. But instead of walking away he laughed, said, 'You'd probably know more than me. I don't read a lot.' He stood at the narrow table, still with his shirt off, and shuffled through the books, holding them up in front of me, asking, 'Good? No?' and putting each down when I shook my head. It was a folding card table, red leatherette pinned to the surface, metal hinges holding the legs straight and not one of the books on the table was one I wanted.

When he'd gone through all the books, looking at the covers, holding them up, putting them down, he walked over to the noticeboard on the other wall, stood scanning the torn-off pieces of paper and handwritten cards, while I tried to make sense of the words on the page in front of me. After a while he said, 'Jesus, she's beautiful,' and I felt a stab of envy, familiar and sharp.

He was gazing at a photo not of a woman, but of a boat. And it – she – was beautiful. 'She' because you owned a boat, I suppose, or rode her, or led her. The joke, of course, was that she owned you, and you spent all your money on her. 'You' being a 'he'.

The boat *was* beautiful. *Gloria.* Cloud-white, gleaming, broad glass windows with light bouncing off it. Below the photo was a printed notice:

Cook wanted. International sailing. Passport necessary.
Interviews daily between 2 p.m. and 4 p.m.

As a kid I'd spent glorious summers sailing a small dinghy at the Speers Point Sailing Club. I sailed the club dinghy, heavy-bottomed and with an ancient sail, so worn it could never be fully taut. Saturdays were full of the jangle of rattling stays and the smell of salt, the air slapping at me and at the sail; I could be led by the wind in that little boat and no one could get at me. When high school started, I got too heavy for the club boat and that was the end of sailing, but the song of boat stays and anchor chains has always made me think of hope, of possibility and promise.

I read the notice again. *International sailing. Passport necessary.* I looked up at the plastic clock above the dryers: 12.20 p.m. This was my ticket. At last, my ship had come in.

AT MY MOTHER'S wedding reception, we sat at a long table and were served prawn cocktails and steak Diane. My mother lifted Neil's hand to her lips and raised her glass to the table. She said, 'When I met you, Nellie, I knew that my ship had come in.'

Neil, my mother's husband, was a tiny man, puff-chested, strangely upright, as though held by a piece of string from the ceiling, or from the sky. He'd met my mother at a dance. 'Oh,' she said, 'he could move.' His hand on her back, guiding her around the dance floor while other couples applauded. You look wonderful together, someone said, and my mother caught a glimpse of the two of them reflected in the long dark windows. She was tiny, a match for him. Later, she said this too: 'He made me *laugh*. Oh God,' she said, 'how I laughed with him.' She called him Nellie, as though he were a girl, or a doll, and it left a slight, unpleasant tang in my mouth.

He proposed to her after six weeks. They married two months after that, in a sailing club on the far side of the lake. We're all smiling, in the photo. My brother in his new air force uniform, holding my mother's arm. If it was strange that he gave her away, no one thought to comment. I'm fifteen, my hair bundled up into a tight French braid, twisted under my head, a silky brown dress that I'd bought from the store I worked in after school and on weekends. Even with the staff discount it took me five weeks to pay it off, almost the entire length of my mother's engagement.

The day of the wedding was the second time I'd met him.

When they married, my mother and her new husband, she carried a Gideon's New Testament, topped with florist's ribbon and a bunch of lavender. It makes me ache, now, looking at the photo of her holding the Bible that she had no belief in, the too-shiny ribbon, the rose at her throat. Poverty, in our family, was not only the absence of money or land but a poverty of the imagination. My imagination, on the other hand, was already peopled with phantoms, ghosts, with hopeful heroines, with schoolgirls and rock stars. Every night I tried to map my way out of the world I was born into.

But at fifteen my future seemed to be mapped for me with my mother's marriage to this broken man. The second bedroom in his shack-like house was full to the ceiling with boxes, cases, old papers, and there was no room for me. Cardboard boxes with the names of places and assorted dates scrawled on the outside tottered in the place that a bed should be. Later, after Neil's death, I would discover that these boxes were full of stunning black-and-white photographs taken in Korea during the Korean War. Posted there as a young photographer, barely twenty years old, Neil took careful, loving photos of handsome soldiers gazing into the sun, their eyes narrowed. There were images, too, of Korean women and men, captured laughing together with the grasslands behind them. When I finally see these images, I am unable to reconcile the loving gaze behind the camera with the man I knew, the man my mother married.

As she left the sailing club where the wedding reception was held, my mother kissed me on the cheek and whispered, 'Just give us a few weeks and we'll fix it up. It'll be lovely.'

I moved into the unlined shed at the back of the house, on top of a crooked concrete slab. The glass-slatted windows didn't close, so the shed was full, always, of mosquitoes or cold night air. Every few days in that short period when I lived in the shed, my mother's husband would drink too much whisky and have a blowout. Sometimes this blowout involved staggering through the house, breaking something and falling into bed. Sometimes it involved shouting, fist-brandishing, his face turning a mottled claret. Often, the fist would be raised and sometimes it would land on me.

They tore the house down, the two of them, when I moved to the hostel, where I borrowed old copies of *Penthouse* from one of the other residents. Skipping over the photos of pink labia and finger-wetted nipples, I tore out the psychedelic pictures and coloured illustrations, gluing them all over my wall, and I got ready for my last year of high school, the year that, apparently, would determine my future.

I came to their house, or at least the site it was to be built on, a year or so after they were married. They'd moved into the exposed shed while they tore down the old shack – its wine-coloured walls painted by Neil's second wife in a drunken flourish, before the drunken flourish and despair that ended with her suicide. Neil and his brother built the new house, while my mother worked double shifts at the hospital and cooked meals on a camping stove. One night, after sharing a flagon of riesling with other residents of the hostel, I phoned my boyfriend from the hostel payphone and asked him to drive me out to the house, or rather to the shed and the building site.

My boyfriend asked if I was sure that was a good idea. He was kind, steady, loyal; a certain sort of salvation through those years. His wall was plastered with posters of Madonna; he could lip-sync perfectly to Annie Lennox singing 'Sweet Dreams', and knew all the words to 'I Will Survive'. Drunkenly, I explained that he should be supporting me, not totally criticising me and all my choices, and if he didn't want to drive me I was sure that Peter, the unemployed surfer who'd shared the riesling with me, would drive me out there.

My boyfriend picked me up outside the hostel fifteen minutes later and drove the forty minutes to my mother's new house. When he stopped the engine outside, he said, 'Are you sure – ?'

I held my hand up in a stop sign. I knew a good idea when I had one in front of me.

My mother was in the shed, cooking on the camping stove. Her husband and his brother sat on camping chairs, each of them holding a beer bottle in a stubby holder. Neil's read: *If you have to ask, don't ask.*

I stood swaying, looking at the stubby holder.

Neil didn't get up. He said, 'What are you doing here?'

My mother, looking at Neil but speaking to me, parroted him. 'What are you doing here?'

I waved my arms, windmill-like.

'Come to see the new house.'

'You've been drinking. You're drunk.' Neil pointed his stubby holder at me, the reds of his eyes glinting accusingly.

I lifted my hand in a 'cheers' gesture and slurred, 'Takes one to know one.'

Long before he twirled my mother about the dance floor, Neil had four daughters. Like little steps, a year or two apart. Golden-haired, gleeful, fat-kneed. I imagine them, hands linked together, their piping voices calling up at him. He had the four of them in his car one night as he drove up to an intersection. Four fat-kneed girls giggling in the back seat. Seatbelts? Probably not. It's dark, no streetlights beaming down, and the whistle of wind outside, rattling the windows of the thinly built houses. It's hard to see on the corner, and Neil noses out. The middle girl is asleep, her chin resting on her sister's shoulder. Chocolate milk stains make a pattern on her T-shirt. Earlier, she giggled so much at her father being a monster that the chocolate milk spurted down her shirt and he raised his voice, then, said there was no time to get a clean shirt. Honestly, he'd said. Little grub. Now, as she sleeps in the car, he puts his foot on the accelerator, pulls out from the corner. He doesn't see the other car.

He pulled out – this is the story told to me by my mother – and an American actor (it's important that he's American, that he's famous, that he has all the things that Neil does not) slammed into the side of his car. Two of the girls were killed.

I don't know, have never known, whether the drinking and the bile came before his girls were killed or after. I don't know, will never know, if he was sober on the night they were killed. Two little girls survived. His marriage ended.

Perhaps, like my mother, and like me, he was waiting for something better. Sitting on the dock of the bay, waiting for his ship to come in, not feeling fine.

I WAS GLAD, when I walked into the marina, that I'd plaited my hair. It made me feel clean and European at the same time. I belonged there, that was what I wanted to believe.

This was not like the dock. The dark green of the water was the same, yes. The land was the same, yes. But, shimmering off the water, a parade of white yachts and gleaming cruisers. At the end of one pier, a woman in a white tank top hosed down a shining hull. I peered at the side of the yacht. *Gloria*. Beautiful. The boat, and the woman. I was not like them. I'd learned this early on, and the lesson was repeated throughout my schooldays, then during my brief sojourn at Sydney University, where I'd arrived after miraculously completing secondary school with the grades to get there, before realising that I had no idea how to sustain myself in that environment, how to stay, how to thrive. Always, somehow, outside. Temperament, sometimes, but more often it was the sharp slice of class.

When I'd moved into my first share house in my first semester of university, I believed myself to be the same as the two boys I moved in with. Simon and Kris: med students who'd taken a gap year to travel around Europe. Unbelievably exotic. I studied them carefully, believing that I could be like them, failing to see the ladder of inherited privilege and assumption that they were lifted on daily. They thought it was cute that I worked weeknights in a tacky illegal Greek gambling club and on weekends worked till 3 a.m. at a Lebanese nightclub; cute that the late hours led to skipping lectures, missing events, failing exams. The people I served drinks with until the early hours liked me, and I liked them. Their work ethic, their forced good cheer: these felt familiar. But I was not like them either. When I returned to visit the house my mother lived in with her bantam-chested husband, I sat in the sun in the back garden, parked under the frangipani tree, trying to read while my stepfather disappeared into his shed, cradling bottles of gin, whisky and rum. In that world, I was a freak, a Matilda who'd sprung from – what? Some strange seed of hope and of words; the gift of found and borrowed books. My language and my expectations, both were hybrid.

The woman standing on the front of the yacht flicked her white shirt back. Sun blistered my sandaled feet, my toenails with their chipped red polish like fruit against the brown of the leather. At the side of the pier, a school of whiting swirled, moving up and down the length of it, twisting in and out of the centre. There was a pattern to it, to their swimming, I knew that. But I couldn't see it. I could only see chaos or, when I looked closer, individual fish. Thin threads of silver, glints of green by the gills. Above me, the white shirt flicked again, and I lifted my hand to shield my eyes from the glare.

'I'm here about the cook's job?' I tried to smile like someone who belonged on this yacht, someone who had grown up leaping from bow to stern wearing designer maillots; a girl with long tanned legs, a girl with straight white teeth, a girl with the right to be there.

I was not that girl. Also, I was not a cook.

The woman leaped down from the boat in one movement and landed on the deck beside me, her knees bending slightly, making barely a thud.

'Hi.' She held out a long hand. A gold anchor hung off the delicate chain circling her wrist; with her hand outstretched, the anchor pointed down to my toes.

I touched the tip of it. 'That's beautiful.'

'Sue gave it to me. Sue and Joe own the boat.'

'Oh, you're not – ?'

'I'm the nanny.'

'They have kids?' Expansive, gleaming, the *Gloria* shone above me. Salty saliva, the taste of lust, filled my mouth as I imagined being the child of such riches. Having a nanny. Living on a yacht. I thought about the boys in Sydney; their easy assumption that their parents would pay a deposit on a house, help them travel. I thought, too, of their seamless, unquestioning belief, both of them, that they were the product of their own work and ambition.

'Two little ones. Sue's just gone up to the marina store. She'll be back in ten.'

'Okay.' I tried a smile. 'I'm Kacey.'

'Like Casey Kasem and the American Top Forty?'

'No. Like KC and the Sunshine Band.'

'Cool.' She stretched her legs out in the sun, toes pointed so that she made a perfect arrow. Her shirt was crisp and clean, like an advertisement. 'Sun's lovely, isn't it?'

'Where are the kids?' I could be a nanny, I thought. Looking after two little kids. How hard could it be? I'm not sure what I intended – to launch the beautiful one into the school of whiting? Encourage her to apply for the cook's job? I stretched my legs out like hers and leaned back, head up to the sun.

It was always like this, watching the others under my lashes, trying to learn how to do it, how to be it, this thing: a girl. Beside this one, my legs looked stumpy, badly shaved. Tanned only in blotches, the thickness of my skaters' thighs loomed next to her *elegant limbs*. I imagined that written up in a magazine interview: her elegant limbs. If I tried hard enough, I could be that, I could be her. I could be anyone but me.

We stretched like that, backs against the hull of the *Gloria*, legs stretched onto the pier, letting the sun bake us. We chatted dozily: she was from Brisbane, had gone to a girls' school, been a nanny ever since. I mostly listened, until footsteps padded along the deck. Above the water, they echoed slightly, a thick muffled sound, a slow music.

'You're here about the job? You're early.' Sue wore white shorts, hair in a neat bob. Plastic shopping bags rustled in her hands. She stepped onto the gunwale and nodded at me. 'Come on up.'

It didn't occur to me to take her bags from her. Lack of initiative. She'd write that down later, for sure. It was my first mistake. My second was staring around the cabin with my mouth open. It's a cliché, but my mouth was actually open. When I was a teenager my father took me out on a single-mast trailer-sailer with some friends; a little bench lined the inside cabin, where we sat peering though the grimy portholes. Perhaps I'd imagined that. In any case, not this: how could I have imagined this wide cabin, the sofas laden with creamy leather cushions, the bolted coffee table, the chrome shelves stacked with books and games, the carpet springing beneath my feet. I had nothing to build this from in my imagination.

'So.' Sue gestured to the sofa and I tried to sit like someone who belonged here, but my legs stuck out in front of me like a child's, and the leather cushions squeaked like farts as I leaned back on them. I smiled without showing my crooked teeth. I did not say, *That was the cushions, it wasn't me*, and nor did I snort with laughter, the way we would have in the house of my childhood. In any of the houses of my childhood.

Sue waved her hand a little more. She wore no jewellery but somehow gave the impression that she did. Her colours matched: an aqua trim in her shorts was, as they say, 'picked up' by a short scarf knotted about her throat. The stripe in her white polo shirt was echoed by her striped belt. Her tanned face was lined around the eyes and the mouth. When she spoke, the crease between her mouth and nose deepened and danced. I couldn't stop watching it, waiting for the next movement.

I said, 'The boat is amazing. It's like being inside a house.'

'Yes,' she said. 'It is. We live half of the time on the boat, because we are in the fortunate position to be able to do so.'

She gave no indication of what enabled them to be in this fortunate position.

I smiled again. She said, 'So,' again, and then we sat in the sort of silence that crackles. I told her I'd sailed as a kid, weekends at the local sailing club, and she raised her eyebrows a little.

She took a pen out of the pocket of her polo shirt and reached behind her to the galley counter (it looked like marble, but surely it wasn't?) to retrieve a small spiral notepad. 'So, Kassie, is it?'

'Kacey. Like the Sunshine Band.' For some reason, I added, 'I like to sing,' as though my ability to spout disco tunes would keep her and her family entertained on the sea. I wanted to be on this boat, though. I wanted to dive from it, to disappear on it.

She smiled, teeth showing. Said, 'Have you brought a résumé with you?'

It had not occurred to me that I would need a résumé. I shook my head and spoke hurriedly. 'I cooked a lot for my family growing up.'

She tapped the pen against the table. Short nails, unpainted. 'Why was that?'

'Sorry?'

'Why did you cook growing up?'

Why would you not? Instead I kept babbling. 'I worked in an ice-cream shop and then lots of cafés, cooking and waitressing.'

I'd never cooked anything in any café, ever, and when I made cappuccinos they were usually served with inadequate froth and half of the coffee slopped over the side.

'What sorts of things would you propose cooking for us?'

It may seem astonishing that I had not prepared anything, that I had put no thought into how I was to get this job which would finally, unalterably, change my life. But this was how I lived; it was how I got through school, how I failed to get through university, how I swam from job to job. No one had ever told me: prepare. Put the work in. I was falling through life, a dandelion spore drifting and landing wherever, whenever.

What would I cook? What did people cook? What did they eat? What did proper adult humans, people who took care of themselves and others, people who did not huddle under their bedclothes weeping with shame – what did those people eat?

'Casserole.'

Sue glanced around as though someone were about to burst in, tell her what a joke this was, how funny it was. She said, 'We have no budgetary restrictions.' Her mouth made a little twist, as though she were holding in an unexpected surge of vomit.

And again, I could not comprehend how such a thing could be possible. What did that even mean, no budgetary restrictions? Who had unlimited money? And what would they eat?

When I was fifteen, I met Daniel. He was thin, with eyes sunk deep in his face. If I half-closed my eyes and looked at him through a certain kind of mental filter, he looked soulful, like an English pop star. He looked, through that blurred filter, like the sort of boyfriend a proper girl would have. He was perhaps nineteen, maybe twenty. I met him at a pub; he bought me a port and Coke and asked if he could take me to dinner the following weekend. Daniel was, in every respect, a proper gentleman.

The following weekend, he collected me in his car. It had electric windows and I gleefully pressed the buttons to make them go up and down until we arrived at the restaurant, Dino's. He'd dressed up: a tie, a suit. Cufflinks. He was the most dressed-up person in the room. It was one of those restaurants with a mezzanine: a semicircle of tables raised slightly above a lower floor. Like, perhaps, a ship's dining room. It reminded me, anyway, of *The Poseidon Adventure*. We were led, by a waiter wearing a black bow tie, to a table looking down over the city. White tablecloths, made of real cloth. I said, 'This is lovely.'

Daniel raised his hand to the waiter – it was clear to me that he'd practised doing this, alone in his room – and he said, 'It's just a little place I like to come to sometimes.' But when I asked him where the bathrooms were, he didn't know. Later, after I'd had a Benedictine and Coke and half a glass of Blue Nun, a woman with dark curly hair piled on top of her head like Carmen Miranda came in with a basket of roses over her arm. Daniel wanted this to be the most romantic night ever. He'd practised. He'd tried so hard. When he asked me if I wanted a rose, I shook my head just a little, and when he asked again, adding, 'Yes, you do,' I nodded, because it seemed clear that this was what was supposed to happen. He was supposed to want to buy me a rose in a little plastic sheath, and I was supposed to want it. All of it – Dino's, the tablecloths, the car, the rose – this was what girls wanted, what all the girls I knew wanted.

Later, when my mother asked me breathlessly about the date, I said, 'We had a fight,' because that was easier than trying to explain. There was nothing wrong with Daniel. There was something wrong with me.

But that restaurant was the most sophisticated place I had been. And in that moment, I remembered what was on the menu.

'Beef Wellington.'

Sue twisted her mouth again, looked down at her notepad, and then back at me. 'And how would you make it?'

'Just, um, the usual way.'

'Well, I don't cook, so what would your usual way be?'

Outside, the melodic rattle of stays and anchor chains beat time to the wind. I sat back on the leather sofa, making it fart again. Sue raised her eyebrows. 'Kassie? How would you make the beef Wellington?'

I gave the cabin a final, adoring gaze. 'With beef.'

Outside, on the pier, the sun kept burning, and I felt nauseous at what I'd lost. A blister was forming on top of my toe. I bent over to stab at it, to see if I could find some satisfaction in popping it, in watching the warm liquid seep out, leaving only the flap of skin. But it would not be popped; it remained glassy and valiant, keeping its scar completely contained.

OUT ON THE ROAD, I struggled to figure out which way to go, how to find my way back to the lodge. Away from the marina, Darwin was a series of squat buildings. North or south, left or right; I had no idea where the lodge was. Across the road, a few cars pootled past; a fat, bearded man called out the window of one of them, 'Wanna fuck?' I shook my head, and he stuck his finger up, adding, 'Fuck off, you fat slag.'

At least on that side of the road someone might stop, offer me a ride – hopefully without the invitation to fuck or the additional commentary on the size of my arse.

In my second year of high school, I had returned after the summer break with a spectacular new pair of breasts. Presumably they'd been quietly growing all through the previous year, but I'd been oblivious to it. Summer arrived and, like well-watered flowers, they bloomed. Boys at school who had previously been my friends trailed behind me every day singing, 'Am I Ever Gonna See My Feet Again?' They thought it was hilarious. I walked with my head down. They were my friends. They wanted to make each other laugh, that was all. But each day my face grew hotter and my anger grew deeper until, midway through the term, I stopped, turned and shrieked, 'FUCK OFF!' I'd never said those words out loud. I'd never shouted at these boys, or at any boys. The three of them

– I can see their faces and bodies but strain to remember their names. One was tall and gangly, his legs permanently bent, like a spider's legs, his arms in constant motion, his red hair a tangle of enthusiastic curls. In first year, he broke the state record for the eight-hundred-metre sprint. Peter something. And another one, older than he should have been, already with the thin trace of a moustache and jokes borrowed from his father. He had an old man's name, too, something like Fred, or Frank. He had broken no records, but the year before he had made me laugh every day while we ate lunch together. And a short, skinny boy with a semi-permanent grin on his face, who wore a singlet under his school shirt; trying always to please the other boys, the teachers, the girls, anyone. Each of them stopped and drew back as though I'd thrown water on them.

And then they stopped. They stopped singing. They stopped following me. They stopped talking to me. I returned to the state of invisibility from which my breasts had briefly called me. And I was lonely.

After the car drove past on that Darwin road, the silence felt the same as it had back in high school. A limp echo of something that wasn't desire, wasn't hatred, but had something of both in it.

Growing up as a girl, there were countless cars, countless boys and men, shouting their approval or disdain, commenting one way or another. Sometimes from cars, sometimes from footpaths. At thirteen, or maybe fourteen, Lisa O'Daniel and I walked the length of the main road in our town counting the times men told us they liked our tits, or walk, or hair or smile. We got two points for that. If a man asked us to smile or said, *Hello, sweetheart/gorgeous/baby*, that was one point. A plain *hello* only got half a point. We got to twenty points by the time we arrived at the main shops, and then Lisa suggested we split up. She'd walk on one side of the road, me on the other, and we'd count our own points and see who won. But I was bored with the game by then and, anyway, the handsome pony-tailed man who'd kept his eyes on my bra-less top while I walked had somehow unsettled me and I wanted to go home. The bus trip was long and lonely, though, and all the way back I stared out the window, hoping that one of the men on the bus would say something about how pretty I was. Just to each other, perhaps, but loud enough for me to hear.

There were other men in cars, many, always. The men who drove down the streets, leaning out of the window, calling, 'Show us your tits!' A compliment? An invitation? A request?

In another city, a car crawled along beside me quietly while I limped on a sprained ankle, keeping my eyes on the ground, trying not to antagonise.

Once, after the trial, I'd borrowed Sylvie's bicycle. I thought it might return me to myself, to cycle somewhere, to feel strong, to be mobile. I wore a fitted dress, black tights. At a set of traffic lights, I waited, feeling briefly happy, feeling that things might after all be possible. Straddling the bike, my skirt riding up a little, feet ready to hop back onto the pedals. A man walked in front of me, glanced down and said, 'Nice cunt. I'd ride that.' I stood, winded. The man strolled away, indifferent. And then I started to ride after him, calling for him to wait, to answer a couple of questions. The man ran. He ran down a lane and, when I followed him, he scrambled over a fence. And all I wanted was to ask this: What do you want to happen? What response do you want from me, from the other girls, when you shout your little cock-calls? But he could not, would not answer me; he ran as though I brandished a knife.

Now, there was just silence, and the occasional car blasting past, a shred of music floating behind it, a surge of dust pluming and settling. I stood on the verge, thumb out, hopeful, trying to make my arse look smaller by leaning slightly forwards and standing half on tiptoes. It's a trick I learned from *Dolly* magazine. Hurts your back but it's worth it. Ants crawled across my feet and then my ankles, taking little bites out of my flesh, while I stood mesmerised, just watching. Even when tiny specks of blood appeared, I stood staring down at them swarming, unable to stamp my feet or raise my hand, just watching till the blood came.

After a while I started walking in the direction that most of the cars were going in, turning around when I heard a car coming near so that they wouldn't see my fat arse before my face. I remembered a girl telling me – she thought it was hilarious – about her boyfriend who'd stopped to pick up a girl hitchhiking, then when she turned around, said, 'Nah, no fricken way,' and drove off. The girl who told me the story had dark curly hair that sat in a thick fringe down over her eyes, so all you could see were these black lashes, like a tiny little awning. I'd hated her telling me the story, hated that she sided with her boyfriend and not the girl. But I'd also felt a sort of relief that it hadn't happened to me and so, when the girl shook her thick hair and called the unknown girl a stupid slut, I'd stood silently, watching those thick lashes and the trace of mascara that fell onto her cheeks, making black marks below her eyes. Two dots, like a snake bite.

Disappointment curdled in my gut, but deeper than disappointment was the sure and certain knowledge that this was what I deserved: a rebuff, failed hope, the dull scuffs of dust on the road. Gravel made a percussive scrape under my toes with each kick of my foot, an angry maraca reminding me of my nonsense. With each scrape I examined my own ridiculousness, sifting examples from the gravel as though panning for gold, fool's gold. That brief and foolish hour when

I had believed myself to be the girl who could leap from that gleaming deck, when I'd imagined myself in a white bikini, smoothly shaved legs, concave stomach, stretched in the sun while sails curved above me in a perfect arc; when I'd allowed myself to hope, to believe I could escape and become, as Sylvie said, something different, something better.

I walked back to Lameroo Lodge, the steam sticking in my throat, clouding my head. The locals talked about the build-up like it was a living thing, an animal lurking on the periphery of the town, waiting to draw blood. But I could feel it, now, the air straining, swelling with humidity. Dogs I passed – a terrier, a retriever, sharing a lead – had their ears down, slinking close to the ground as though waiting for their owner to snap and raise a fist. It was like walking through a wet velvet curtain, the air soggy and sad on my skin, the sky swelling.

The white-blond man was sitting on the front step of Lameroo Lodge when I dragged my feet up. I'd tied my shirt beneath my bra, trying to let some air on to my skin. He was on his own, looking down at a notebook, his knees drawn to his chest, and for a minute I just stood and watched him moving his finger across the page like a primary school child. I tried to think of something to say, something that wasn't stupid, something that Dean Moriarty might say, something cool. I said, 'Hey.'

When he smiled, one eye closed slightly, making his face look smaller. And when he said, 'Do you want to get a drink?', I felt the disappointment that had wedged in me begin to float away.

I SPENT TWO DAYS looking for more signs for boats on the noticeboard, but there weren't any. I had no money left and I still didn't have a plan, or not a proper one. Sylvie had given me a silver bracelet to remember her. It was an antique, passed down through her family, and before she got on the plane she took it off and put it in my hand; I'd always loved the bloom of the two rubies against the silver. I took it to the pawnshop on the corner of the mall, and a blond-bearded man gave me enough to pay for three more nights at Lameroo Lodge. When he handed me the money, his hand was damp. A piece of pastry had wedged in his beard, below his mouth, and when he spoke the pastry piece wagged up and down like a tail, or a sheep's dag. I said, 'Don't sell it. I'll be back for it. It's a loan, okay? A loan.'

He knew that I would not be back.

I didn't feel lighter, or richer, when I left.

Instead of walking back towards Lameroo, I turned the other way along the road and took the long walk to the mooring basin – the Duck Pond – in case another gleaming yacht might show up, looking for an ill-equipped cook who didn't know how to make beef Wellington.

Metal frames cut across the sky; trawlers docked alongside each other, their high frames reaching up. More than anything, it made me think of a line of crucifixes: that image of Christ on the hill, the crosses silhouetted against the sky. Ropes and pulleys jangled in time with the lilt of the wind, the call of the harbour. Salt mixed with the tangy smell of fish, sharp and strangely sweet.

Raw fish, guts, salt, the turn of prawns: it was all there in the smell. Underneath my sandaled foot, a squish; the head of a prawn, its black eye a savage, desperate bead. I wiped it from underfoot, looking away. There were no beautiful boats looking for cooks, or nannies, or deckhands. There was just the faint wind, making the chains on the boats jangle like church bells.

On the walk back to Lameroo there was no song of boat stays, just the dull whine of occasional traffic and the pad of my feet on the road, and then on the grass outside the lodge. I saw the bag – made by his aunt, or his mother, or an older cousin in suburban Cairns – before I saw him, bright Hobbytex colours calling, *hello*, *hello*. He raised his hand, grinned as though we were old friends, as though we knew each other and were not merely people who had stripped naked and had sex in a shower cubicle after drinking too much bourbon. We'd torn each other raw, tumbling from shower to empty dorm room, throwing each other against any surface we could find, and I felt that I was riding a wave I'd waited for too long to arrive. But there in the open light of the Territory sun I felt stupidly overwhelmed by the self I'd been in the shower cubicle, in the dorm room, in the corridors. Her desire was unseemly. I'd learned that from the trial: that I should be a more contained kind of girl, a more sober kind of girl.

Raised high, his hand made a flag, beckoning me to land. I smiled back at him and sat on the square of grass he patted.

Beside him, there was a darker, thinner version of himself. Curls, wide eyes, wide cheeks. But rather than white-haired, sand-skinned, the younger version – sitting cross-legged, grinning at me – was black-haired, skin dark like my brother's, eyes cow-brown. 'This is my brother Karl,' he said.

I waited for him to tell me his own name, but clearly he thought I would remember. So then I waited for Karl to call his brother something and, after a while, he did.

'Robbie said you might be here.'

'He did?' He'd *talked* about me? Jesus.

Meeting Karl was a lucky accident. Courtesy of his brother, Karl arrived in my life suddenly and straightforwardly, the way he arrived everywhere. He was the most straightforward, the most guileless person I'd ever met.

It's rare for me to think of him now. A year ago or so, a boy passed me, skinny in a Bob Marley T-shirt, his hair long, curls twirling about his face, then Karl popped into my head with a rush of tenderness, a desperate wish to know he was safe, well, happy. He will be. He'll be skippering something gorgeous. He'll be hunting and winning. With his surname long since forgotten, I tried googling 'Karl. Trawler' but got nothing.

'Karl. Timor Sea. Skipper.'

Still nothing.

'Karl. Trawler. Robbie.'

Nothing. He has disappeared, like so many others, into the gulf or the waters that surround it.

Karl and I sat in the dining hall of Lameroo Lodge, and he told me this: that I could get myself out of the unholy mess I was in, if I jumped on a trawler with him and went out as a cook. He was waiting for a boat to come in with a new skipper, a new crew that he was going to join. He'd missed the start of this season and the last half of banana season – the short months of mad frenzied catching before the start of the build-up – because his mother died. He didn't want to talk about it. His usual boat had gone out with a different first mate so now he was going out on the *Ocean Thief*. The irony of the name, *Ocean Thief*, did not escape me. I'd topped my school in English; I knew what irony was.

He unfolded a map and spread it across the table, right next to the small shredded one I'd carried in my backpack all this way, taking it out at every truck stop, recording the route with a ballpoint pen, in tiny neat crosses, like a treasure map.

I traced the rim of the Gulf of Carpentaria with my finger. My nails were square and bitten to the quick – even now I struggle with my hands, struggle to make them look like lady-hands, manicured, soft. Once, a year or two after the gulf, a boyfriend ran his thumb along the rise between my palm and my index finger. Really, even by then, he was an ex-boyfriend. I'd ended it for complicated reasons and then wished I hadn't. I was still desperately in love with him and I hoped the handholding was the instant that would lead us back to each other, lead him to forgiveness and recapitulation. Instead, he said, 'Your hands are like dinosaur skin, aren't they? What did you do to them?'

For (again, complicated) reasons, I'd never told him about the *Ocean Thief*. I'd never told him about the nights on watch, about the shift of water across the Arafura Sea, about the storms and the losses. I'd never told him about the trial, not any of that. I'd arrived in his life on my way to being fully formed, a woman. I didn't want him to know me as the messy girl I'd been. Anyway, I knew then, when he looked at my hands and saw only abhorrent rough skin, I knew we were properly over. And that was one more thing to blame the gulf for.

Although later I'd know that it was one more thing to thank it for.

We'd woken on the grass outside Lameroo Lodge: me and Robbie with our legs entwined, his hand on my bare belly, his white curls matted with sleep and humidity. I trailed my finger along his nose, the breadth of it, and then across his eyelashes, white-blond like his hair. He blinked at me; eyes green beneath the pale lashes. Was I allowed to trace my hand over him like this, suggesting ownership?

Somewhere in the background there was a girl down south, studying, waiting for her on-off boyfriend to come back from the top of the country where he had gone to see his baby brother, the sailor, the fisherman, after their mother died. Robbie, smooth-skinned, pale-eyed, his curls like sandstorms – he was the one who was crossing into a different world, a world of books, of suits and ties, while Karl hung from booms and heaved on winches and stank of fish and fuel. Like Karl, Robbie did not want to talk about his mother, about the sudden loss and the gap she left behind.

Heat had already geysered up from the northern rim, sun spreading across the grass like butter. There were no footsteps. Karl arrived unbidden, moving like sunlight, the way he always did. Wet sprinkled down, a spattering of rain, or dew, and the wrinkle of a laugh. Robbie's eyes blinked properly open then, his teeth gleaming with that smile they shared. Above us, Karl shook his head, water spraying out in droplets.

'You're like a dog.' Robbie's hand reached around his brother's ankle, his hand pale against the deep dark of Karl's leg.

The two of them were like shadow negatives of each other: Robbie, steady and softly spoken, his face still, eyebrows raised while he listened carefully. Karl ran at the world, arms open, always moving, a dynamic streak. He lifted his foot, the grey heel hovering over Robbie's face. 'Come on. Up. Got news. And an idea.'

Something red was smeared across the surface of the plastic table. Jam, perhaps, or tomato sauce, just next to Karl's map, unfolded in front of me. *Carpentaria*. Two limbs of land stuck out into the shock of turquoise, the wide expanse of water leading to Asia, leading to Away, leading to Freedom.

Karl pointed to the bite on the map that denoted the far side of the Territory, the space between the Territory and the broad reaches of the west. Bonaparte Gulf. 'That's where we fish for banana prawns.'

Banana prawns: it seemed like a made-up name. Like he was a kid playing at being a working fisherman. Karl kept his finger on the map, moved it across to the wider, longer space between land and ocean, the long tip of Australia butting into the Arafura Sea. 'But here's Carpentaria. Tiger prawns.'

'For real? Tiger as in jungle?'

'I don't think tigers live in the jungle. But, yeah, same name. And those babies will bring in plenty of cash. Anyway, there's some weird shit with this crew. The decky and the mate went AWOL. I don't know what went down, but the cook's gone too.'

'Is the cook always a she?'

He looked at me blankly. 'The cook is always a girl. Do you want to do it? Robbie said you were looking for a boat gig. You make more money on a trawler.'

Michael, the ride who delivered me to Darwin while sliding his hand along the crease of my leg, he'd talked about trawlers and cooks, made my head swim with memories of the docks. I'd made a mess of things. I'd made a mess of everything. But maybe, after all, there was a way. Even if I couldn't cook.

'Here,' Karl said, his finger pointing out the borders of the country and the aquamarine expanse that surrounded it. 'We fly into Groote Eylandt – there – and leave from here, and then we're roughly in this area here.'

'How long?'

'Four months – if we get a good catch.'

'How much?'

'Ten grand.' He grinned. 'If we get a good catch. You make more in banana season, but that's pretty much over now.'

'I'd come back with ten grand? Is it dangerous? For a girl?'

He knew what I was asking. He looked down at his hands, his nails tapping on the tabletop. Then he said, 'Everything's dangerous sometimes. But if you come out on this boat, I'll make sure nothing happens to you. No one will touch you.'

Ten grand. My mouth watered at the thought of it. I could feel the folded notes in my hand. Enough to buy a ticket, a steed, a lance, a castle. Enough to get me out, make me new, make me one of the great ones.

All those promises of gold and silver, the riches that would get me off this large island and get me to somewhere, anywhere else, the place where everything would be different. England, perhaps, where I would find my mettle. Why not there, in Fantasy Pre-War Upper-Middle-Class England? Home of Maisie of the Fourth and Susie of the Upper Sixth; refuge for bookish loners.

I knew this: the further I could go from the self I was, the more I could become my other self, the self I knew I could be. I was making this from nothing, from the tools only of imagination.

I would, if I could, start a bonfire and I would burn all that I had been, all that I had been told I was, all that I'd been born to. I'd be the firestarter.

DUST COVERED MY FEET, my calves, my hands. Red tracks had formed under my knees though I'd barely made it from the small plane to the wire fence at the end of the tarmac. White paint proclaimed the words: *Groote Eylandt Airport*. Heat merged with the fumes of the plane, buckling the air, rippling it in the way that would signify a change in time, or memory, in a cheesy film. Karl bobbed beside me, his wild curls bouncing; he was like a puppy, leaping on the dirt, ready to be let off the leash, waiting for the smell of salt.

Salt water fixes everything: tears, sweat or sea. Someone said it. I believed it.

Rows of wooden seats curved around the wire fence, making a semicircle, a smile echoed by the toothless smile on the face of the old fella standing at the gate. Hair washed of colour, rainbow shorts sagging at his knees. He leaned against the wire, watching the dribble of passengers walk down the stairs and across the dirt, his eyebrows thick roads on his face. When we came close, he whipped his hand out and rested it on my shoulder. 'All right, mate?' I nodded, but before I spoke, he'd moved on. His eyes were on Karl and a stream of words came from him, musical and mysterious. Karl lifted his hand in an indifferent wave, but the man yanked him inside the gate, ferrying him to the gathering beneath the shelter. The toothless smiling semicircle of seats was peopled with women in flowery

116

frocks, loose shifts sprinkled with blooming reds, yellows, greens. Five or six women talked over each other, laughter swelling now and then like a river, washing away the sandy banks with its overflow. One woman threw her head back and guffawed, her feet planted wide, her arms flung up in abandon. Her laugh surged and settled, an ebbing wave, and she was like a battered surfer, her arms resting on her knees, her head shaking as though that gut-rocking glee had drawn everything from her.

Watching her, a memory came of my mother, sitting at a table with her women. She was the first in our suburb to divorce. Somehow, she found a small tribe. I suppose she found them through the hospital, where she'd managed to get a job as a nurse's aide. Even as a child I could see the electricity, the flow of energy that zinged through her with the opening of the world of work. Until the years when shift work and poor pay wore her down, this world – the hospital, the gathering of women in the staffroom cackling and chattering – was a door to another world, no less magical than the wardrobe that the Pevensie children found themselves in before their entrance to Narnia. Even with its emergencies and buzzers and demands, even with Christmas Day after Christmas Day spent in hospital staffrooms without her children, this world was a sanctuary for her, and the women she found in it were her gatekeepers.

Her little gathering of women would happen weekly, their arms resting on the laminate table, their hands touching, their laughter echoing off the walls, and always falling away with that hahaHAHAHAHAWwwwwoooh dear, and the wiping away of tears. Thelma, with her many chins and endless parade of kaftans, beautiful blonde Maureen, and Russian Nadia, always dressed in white, with gold rings flashing on her hands: the most exotic woman I'd ever seen, with the best laugh in the world.

Until now.

This woman was skinny, but with muscular arms, the sinew visible from shoulder to elbow. Her feet were bare, with a pair of plastic sandals plonked in the dirt beside her. When she laughed, her whole body rocked, her feet kicking at the dirt, her legs swinging back and forth. Red hydrangeas made a pattern the length of her smock. She stopped her laugh suddenly, like a tap being flicked off, and reached out her hand to Karl, the way the old man did. Karl grinned his grin at her, and she said something to him in her own language. Karl shook his head and she switched to English. 'You comin' home, boy?'

Unfazed, Karl shook his curls at her. 'Nup.' He lifted his chin, gesturing away from the seats, away from the road. 'Going out fishing, Aunty.' His words ran together, so that it sounded like *garnoufishinarny*.

Her hand curled tightly on his wrist. 'Where're your mob from?'

He did the strange tilt with his chin again, said, 'Down west.'

'You belong down there?'

He shrugged; she let go of his wrist. Where do you belong? Who do you belong to? I thought of my own traipsing across the map, my landless walk. There was no land that belonged to me, none that I belonged to, and no one who would claim me as theirs. I belonged only to myself. The voice in my head, chanting this, was defiant, chin up, fist up, loud. But perhaps there was an echo, just one, of a trailing sigh, like the rocking women. Wooo-oh dear; a basin of loss that sat beneath that chiming defiance. I wasn't conscious of wanting to belong – but I was aware of my disconnect from home, my disconnect from country.

I sat on one of the empty benches. When Karl plonked himself beside me, I asked, 'Why'd you call her Aunty?'

'Respect.'

'But you respect me –'

He let out a short laugh, like a bark.

' – and you don't call me Aunty.'

'You're not . . .'

'What?'

'You're not old enough.' He paused, shuffled his feet and added, 'And you're not my people.'

Again, that chanting voice. *I have no people.*

On a day much later than this, sitting with Karl on the bow deck, watching a flock of terns on the boom, I will ask him, 'Why is Robbie white? What's his story?'

And Karl's face will close off to me; he will shift his legs in front of him so that he is turned away from me as he replies, 'Why are you? What's *your* story?'

On that occasion, with the warmth of the deck beneath my legs, I will think of the slow days of coiling rope, twisting them into order, each thread connecting to another. And I will say, 'Got no story, got no people.' And I'll believe it to be true. No land, no people, no story, no worries.

Only the last bit isn't true.

There was no closed-in building in the tin-shed airport, apart from the tin-bound toilets labelled *Lady* and *Man*. We waited beneath the hand-painted *Luggage Collection* sign until a woman wearing a straw hat the same colour as her face wheeled a caged trolley out in front of us. Perspiration patches made maps of New Zealand beneath her arms, beneath her breasts, on her belly. When she lifted her hand to remove the hat, her wide orange T-shirt rode up to her bare thighs. Another sign read *Town Bus Here*.

Leaning in to reach for my pack, I glanced up and saw him on the other side of the road, inside the tin bus shelter. Wearing loose khaki shorts and a matching shirt, a grey-haired man sat with his legs spread wide, so wide that I could see his testicles poking out. Round and pink – even from that distance there could be no mistake. While I watched, the man widened his legs and looked up at me, grinning. I could see the crimson tip of his tongue sliding between his teeth.

How do they know we will keep our mouths closed? How do they know we will simply turn away, these men? How do they know, have always known, that I will take the mortification into myself and feel the blaze on my cheeks and keep my eyes on my feet while I walk away? Mouth closed, face burning, bile in the stomach. This is what it's like to be a girl, to be this girl.

The high school in Warners Bay was a series of brick buildings, square and unyielding, arranged in random patterns, squatting wherever they landed. A Block. B Block. D Block. Prison titles. Prison architecture. And from that prison Lisa O'Daniel and I walked home most afternoons in our first year of high school, making each other collapse with laughter, having to stop and rest our hands on our own knees like old men, losing the ability to speak, losing breath.

We only ever saw the man under the car. We never saw his face, only his legs. Most afternoons he'd be there at the time we walked past, under his black Holden, his King Gees hitched up, his testicles – and sometimes his penis – peeping neatly out the bottom of the shorts. The first time, Lisa glanced down and squeezed my hand. We stopped, giggled, and walked on. We were twelve. We told each other, told ourselves, that this man was hilarious, that his dick was simply a gross joke.

We saw him – or, rather, his testicles, and sometimes his mottled penis – four or five times after that. We didn't giggle the second time, or the third, just squeezed each other's hands and kept walking, agreeing to silence. The last time we saw the wrinkled package arranged outside the shorts, I stayed silent while Lisa shouted, 'You forget to put your underpants on, you dirty great perv.' Hands on hips, she added, '*Fucking* perv.'

That summer, a man at the Speers Point Sailing Club asked me if I'd like to crew for him during a race. I'd taken myself down to the club, wandering up and down the line of men – mostly men – and older teenagers rigging up their boats, asking each one if they needed a for'ard hand. This man, with a thick spring of dark hair and a gut that curved over his board shorts, said yes. I was quiet during the race, unsure. I remember a yellow sail, and a spinnaker covered in vivid stripes. I remember looking up at it, the spinnaker, full of wind, and glancing across to the man. He was perched on the gunwale, legs wide and that little pinkish package protruding, making a flabby worm on his upper leg, a broad grin on his face, eyes on mine. Was it deliberate? Was it just the unfortunate by-product of having physical bits and pieces that wouldn't stay put? I squeezed my own knees together and chewed on my lip, kept my eyes on the yellow sail until we sailed back to the clubhouse.

We stopped walking home together after that, me and Lisa O'Daniel. I caught the bus home alone instead, staring out the window, burying myself in silence.

At the Groote Eylandt Airport, the town bus arrived, blocking the view of the bus shelter and the testicle display across the road. Karl nudged me. 'You okay?' And I said, yes, I was fine, absolutely fine.

PALE BLUE BUTTED against the horizon, the sky meeting the water, so that the whole seemed like a cerulean wall against which one might crash. Sand had trailed up my calves, into the creases of my knees, down into my socks. A wide groyne extended into the water and, beyond that, the red chute of the mines, cutting up the land. I wanted this to be pretty, I wanted it to be a story of beauty and wonder, and so I squinted towards the blurred horizon and held my hand to the side of my face, blinkering myself, horse-like, from the red rust, the corridor of industry chugging up and down the road. This was the way I lived in that time, blinkering myself, looking only at a narrow field, so I only saw what I wished to see.

The *Ocean Thief* was anchored a few hundred metres out, low waves washing against the hull. Sun glinted off it, and with the trawling arms stretched across the water it had, I suppose, a grandness to it. Bigger than I'd expected, with birds flocking about it, surging and settling like the froth of waves.

The town driver had dropped us with a cheery warning to watch out for crocodiles, but while I tried to keep away from the water Karl cantered up and down the narrow stretch of sand with no care for crocs, waving his arms in a semaphore arc.

There was no answering movement from the boat anchored offshore.

Above us the sun burned brighter, its sweltering call answered by the sand sparking on my feet. I sat under the sprinkling of stingy scrub – trees with berries I couldn't identify, bushes I could not name – and wiggled my shoes off. We waited. The sun got hotter. Karl found an apple in his bag and we ate it bite for bite, swearing in turns. Honestly, it might have been less than an hour, but it felt as if days had passed by the time we heard the low putt of an outboard and saw the nose of an aluminium boat mousing out from the bow of the *Ocean Thief*.

Light glinted off the tinnie as it puttered across the bay. Karl ran to the shoreline, a smudge of crayon against the yellow sand and cobalt sky. Arms semaphoring, his skinny legs beat time while his shout whooped across the water. From my rock perch under the single scrappy tree, I watched the battered tinnie curve around, the bow pointing to land, to us, while Karl leaped and whooped some more. Shadow stretched across my legs, the shapes of the flimsy canopy creating dark trails across my skin. I ran my hand along the lines, tracing the strange language of tree shade written there, curved like the mysterious etchings on silvery scribbly bark. I'm trying, now, to recall my first sighting of a scribbly bark. Did I ever not know that tree, with its smooth trunk interrupted along the length of its body by alien etchings, like strange messages scribbled into the bark?

When, as a ten-year-old girl, I read *Anne of Green Gables*, I tried to harness the romanticism of Anne. In summer, I tried to stand at the base of trees in our yard, embracing the trunks, whispering to them. Even with no audience, I felt foolish; inauthentic, although I did not know the word. But the scribbly bark could always elicit wonder worthy of Anne. There on that beach, the wonder was returned, although the text was written on my body, not on the bark of the tree. Against my back, the bark was scratchy, peeling. The tree was flimsy, unidentified – not even a eucalypt – while I waited for new words, a new life.

Halfway to land, the tinnie made a deliberate turn away from us and headed to the far end of the beach. At the threshold between water and land, Karl stopped jumping and rested his hands on his hips, glaring along the length of sand. Not moving, I called out, 'What's happening?' As though I were a queen on holiday, waiting for a weather update from her servants.

'He's – there's some – I dunno. Maybe it's not ours.' He pointed to the distant rocks, where someone clambered into the hull. From where I stood, the person doing the clambering looked like a small skinny palm tree, a wild batch of branches moving about on top of a thin trunk.

I abandoned my shaded retreat and edged closer to the water, toes well away from the temptation of crocs, and peered at the boat now turning back, puttering away from land before, finally, turning towards us. Unthinkingly, I slipped my hand into Karl's. He said, 'It'll be fine. Seriously. Everything's fine.'

Gradually, the shape of the two people in the boat became clearer. Hand on the tiller, a man with a dark beard stared ahead, a peaked cap over his eyes so that he was just a shadow. Another shape: a wild-haired man. Or a boy? Shoulders like a wire coat hanger, hair making a dark halo. Skin so milky that it reflected the sun.

Karl kept his eyes on the water. As the tinnie came closer, he plastered that wild white-toothed grin on his face, lifted his hand in a salute and stepped knee-deep to grab the gunwale. 'All right? What's the story?'

'Hey. Got your stuff?' It was the bearded man, his lips barely moving.

Karl tried again. 'You the skipper?'

'Yep. Mick.' He lifted a hand, tugged the cap further down over his eyes, and pointed towards the trawler anchored offshore. 'That's home.'

'I'm Davey.' The skinny boy in the bow—I could see now he was definitely a boy—stood up, wobbling. His knees were round orbs, covered in brown scabs.

'Whoa. Steady.' Karl held his hand out, grabbing Davey's elbow.

'Ain't got my sea legs yet.' He smiled at us both, open, seemingly not at all embarrassed by his lack of sea legs.

When the skipper lifted my pack into the tinnie, he grunted at the weight and said, 'You got rocks in here?'

'No,' I said. 'Books.'

He raised his black eyebrows at that. Said, 'You'll be working, not reading.'

I thought about the hundreds of thousands of words gathered in the bottom of that pack, the answers to everything, but I nodded.

Mick started up the outboard and, over the whine of the motor, said, 'You know how to cook?' and I said that of course I did, although I didn't, not really.

I don't know if Karl knew then that Mick had never skippered before, that he'd been given the job by his fleet-owning uncle, but he grinned and said, 'What about you, Mick? You know how to skipper?'

Mick said, 'What? What the fuck's that supposed to mean?'

'Nothing, man. It's a joke.'

'Right.' The skipper smiled briefly and turned the tinnie back towards the *Ocean Thief*, the aluminium hull thudding slightly as we slapped across the swell. My pack bounced with each dip, making a series of dull clunks. The enamel mug I'd strapped to the outside chimed so that all I could hear was the thud and beat of the boat and my pack, and the cymbal chime of my cup making a musical accompaniment. Light glinted off the water in diamonds. White-faced gulls swooped above us, in and out of the glinting light. I let the wind brush my neck, and I watched the sunshine dance. If I tried, I could feel that I was in a film.

WE WERE CLOSE to the water in our little boat, and the trawler loomed up, dark and broad, the words *Ocean Thief* in white on the tip of the bow. It seemed right that I'd be on a boat branded for theft, but I was still trying to find the glory and romance. Broad booms stretched on either side of the hull, crucifix-style, a metal frame soaring above the hull. Scores of seabirds swirled about the booms, grouping and separating, their hopeful squawks drowning out the drone of the outboard.

Mick smiled so that the thick mask of his beard moved sideways; a gold filling glinted in his mouth and I couldn't help but think of pirates. 'Beautiful, huh?'

Karl grinned up at the cobalt mass, his curls whipping about his face, but all I saw were thick mounds of bird poo and great streaks of rust. We scooted about the stern, bumping against the tyres extending the length of the hull. Karl tied us up while the new deckhand and I sat uselessly.

A sunburned face appeared above us, peering over the gunwale. 'You pass me the bags.'

We lifted my pack up and once more there was the joke about the rocks – this time from the voice above me. I wobbled when I stood and had to keep my hand on Karl's shoulder. I stretched, grabbing at a tyre, and stepped into it, then hauled myself onto the *Ocean Thief*. When my bare feet hit the deck, I had to stop myself applauding.

'I am engineer. He calls me Frenchie.' The owner of the voice and the sunburn nodded towards Mick, still sitting in the tinnie.

I said, 'What should I call you?'

'Frenchie.'

'Oi! We're waiting for help down here.'

We scrabbled up and over. First Davey, then Karl and then the skipper, until we were standing in a reluctant circle on the deck. Most of the open space was taken up by an aluminium tray, long and deep, so that we had to skirt it to get to the galley door. Mick nodded towards Frenchie, said, 'This is Frenchie, the engineer. Once you've put your bags in your bunks, I'll give you the tour.' He nodded at each of us in turn, the straggle of crew, and we each gave our names. Something strange sat over us, a heavy discomfort, a nervousness, like we'd arrived too early at a party. Everything smelled of salt, and fuel.

From there, high up on the trawler, the land already looked far away, and I told myself that I was escaping at last. Like Moriarty, like Quixote, like Caulfield, I was embarked, adventuring, starring in my story.

Inside, in the dark nudge of a cabin that was to be mine and mine alone, I dropped my pack against the door. Two bunks nestled against the wall. I squatted down beside my pack and took the books out one by one, lining them up on the narrow shelf carved into the end of the bunk. They made it feel more like a room, like a home. I ran my finger along the spines, grateful that they would be my travelling companions. Outside, the voices of four men merged into one, growling like the low hum of the engine beneath me, merging into one booming bass. When they laughed, the voices bled together, so that all I heard was a bass thud, like a hammer pounding down, bang-bang.

It was womb-like, that cabin: dark, windowless, contained. I unpacked, laying everything out on the bed: stolen Ray-Bans, painstakingly stitched cut-off denims, cute halter tops that I now understood were ridiculous in my new environment. The enamel mug, teal-rimmed and chipped, I wedged on the narrow shelf between the rail of my bunk and the cabin wall. Then I put three pens in it, angling them jauntily, although I had no audience. Two red A4 journals, lined. A toiletry bag full of optimistic creams and unnecessary mascara, sheer lip gloss, nail polish which would chip off with one evening's catch. I wanted this little womb to feel like home, although I had no home, had not had a home for as long as I could remember. Someone in Sydney had given me a silk cloth, red, stitched with black, and I placed that like a coaster, or a 1950s doily, beneath the cup of pens. I'd sketched a picture of Robbie—his narrow nose, his curls – drawing him with a wild puzzle-door opening in his head, though he wasn't complicated, not in the way I'd wanted him to be. I stuck the picture to the wall as a sort of scarecrow: I hoped that the ownership the sketch of a man implied would keep any others from my door.

Outside, I could hear the voices separating, footsteps tapping out over the engine, coughing. Karl called something – the eagerness in his voice recognisable even in the audio murk of engine noise – and the new deckhand, Davey, called back. A rattling on my door then; Karl's voice calling, 'Kacey?' I didn't feel ready for the jostle of people and voices, the wide expanse of sea, the uncertainty of it all, the fear. And I didn't yet understand what it meant to need my own company, to be enriched by it. When I opened the door, Karl's face was beaming, his feet planted wide. It was clear that on this hulk of steel, with the stretch of water outside, he was himself. He nodded at the sketch above my bunk, though if he recognised it as a picture of his brother he didn't say.

'Come on,' he said. 'You need to see where we are.'

And I followed him, ducking my head as I stepped out from the galley to the shelter of the stern deck. The engine was louder there, and I wondered if I'd made one more stupid mistake. Already I wanted to shout at it all to shut up, to stop, to give me the silence and the romance and the grand adventure, yes, that I was there for. Not this grubby industrial roar, the battering of wind on the hull, the shriek behind us. But I followed Karl, clambering behind him up the ladder to the upper deck, sidling around past the wheelhouse until we were on the bow deck, looking down at the way ahead of us. Sun streamed onto the steel, bounced off the glass of the wheelhouse, bounced into my eyes, and the mouth of the gulf opened up ahead of me and if I squinted just so, the way I had with that boy who took me to the restaurant with the beef Wellington, if I squeezed my lashes and looked only at a corner of the frame, my God, after all it *was* the grand adventure. Beautiful, wild, romantic and true.

KEROUAC COULD TAKE his prosepurpleprose and shove it, because there I was, wind in my hair, salt on my skin, the dock and town becoming a small dot behind me while I clambered on the deck. Sun on my hands, on my way to freedom.

The narrow stretch of beach with the stringy scrappy trees disappeared, and then after it the cars behind the car park disappeared, and then the road was a line behind us, and then the stretch of the wide mouth of land grew distant.

Paint flaked on the gunwale, small islands of dark steel emerging beneath the enamel. Karl careened on the stern deck, moving like a piece of the boat. The four of us climbed up to the wheelhouse to join the skipper as we left the wide mouth of the harbour, faces to the blazing horizon.

And then Mick said, 'Dinner?'

I nodded. Yes, dinner would be lovely. It took a blink, a breath, to remember, to understand. I was the person responsible for dinner.

The galley was tiny, suffocating compared to outside. Already listing to one side, the sweep up and down of the galley floor made me queasy. Grey laminate covered the bench, cutting the galley in two: above it, the bars holding everything in place, the clips on the doors, the order. I had no list, no order, no thought. Onions. There were onions. Everything should have onions. And as I chopped, my mouth filled with saliva, and the galley walls squeezed in on me. Inside the galley was filled with the fume of oil and onion, and outside there was sky and sea. Already I was stuck again, contained, held inside, because I was not a knight, not a beat boy, just a girl. Outside, Karl called to Davey, leaping on booms and nets; this was what I imagined, fuelling my imagination with a vague resentment. I did not want to be a cook.

In Sydney, I'd tried to get a job as a labourer, walking from building site to building site in my cut-off jeans. On each site I was laughed off with one look at my soft arms and the curve of my breasts. But I knew a boy in the town I grew up in who had padding on his belly and flab on his arms. He got a job as a brickie's labourer, and I watched his arms grow muscled and his belly hard. That work – being outside, lifting and carting and carrying, and being so tired in your body that you have no room to think, that you are forced out of your head and only your body does the thinking: that was the work I'd wanted. I had knocked on every door I could find and then I put an ad in the local paper: *Work wanted. Nineteen-year-old girl. Strong. Willing.* Did I say I'd do anything? Or just that I'd work hard? I can't be sure of the ratio of naivety to blind hope, the naivety that was hidden deep in me, with my swagger and my sophistication borrowed from books. The day the ad came out in the paper, I perched on a broken stool in the dingy sitting room of the share house, next to the phone, waiting for it to ring. One man called. Would I do *any* work? What did I mean by labouring? What size uniform would I wear? What about on the top? What size on the top? I answered each question, waiting for the job offer that would mean I could pay my rent, while I sketched pictures of flowers in the margins of my journal. When he asked about the size of my top, I hesitated, and only then noticed the panting on the other end of the phone, the words coming out in croaks, the escalating sigh. I disconnected, left the phone hanging by a cord, the disconnect signal pinging into the empty sitting room, while I brushed my teeth and scrubbed my face and squinted at my own stupid self in the fly-spotted bathroom mirror.

Three industrial-sized fridge doors lined the wall in the galley. I stared at the shelves inside: the fresh food sprouting at the bottom of the cool boxes, the jars of pickles and sauces. A pair of legs appeared on the ladder that led up to the wheelhouse, the skipper's bearded face peering down at me. 'All right?'

I nodded. 'Yep. Fine.'

He unfolded himself, so that his head was again out of sight. 'Mick?'

His face appeared again. 'Yep?'

'What would you normally eat?'

He spoke as he moved upwards, so that I could only see his knees, and then his feet. 'Meat. Frenchie took some beef out of the freezer this morning.'

In the sink, I found a plastic container full of chunks of red flesh. I'd stopped eating meat during my time in the hostel in high school – first because I couldn't afford it, and then because I wanted to stop eating, wanted to stop thinking about food, wanted my body to shrink to a tiny acceptable size. Now, I picked out the fat chunks with a fork, flicking the shining squares into the pan of onions and moving them about until they seemed brown. The cupboards had canned tomatoes and so I poured them in and watched it all bubble, making a sour metallic stink in the narrow galley. I burned the rice and scraped the black bits off the bottom of the pan.

Dinner was silent at first, while everyone but me tried to chew the lumps of meat. I'd cooked myself a boiled egg, and a piece of toast. We were squeezed around the table, backs against the walls, with the engine blissfully silent, the fluorescent light blasting cold white on our faces. Eventually, Frenchie said, 'What did you do to this meat? You have destroyed any flavour. This is – ' he waved his fork at me ' – this is not good. This is very bad.'

Karl swallowed, put his fork down and grinned at me. 'It isn't horrible. It's – I mean – I'm usually more hungry than this.'

Davey stared at his plate. Bravely, he took another mouthful, then smiled. 'It's okay. It's fine.'

Frenchie slid out from the table, legs first, round belly following. He opened the fridge door and stuck his head deep inside, rustling and harrumphing, until he emerged with a jar of something and a pot of herbs – parsley, and something dark and leafy. We sat like children, hands on laps, while Frenchie chopped and pounded and mixed, finally presenting a bowl of something green and garlic-fragrant. Tenderly, he scooped spoonfuls onto the plates of gelatinous meat, then stood watching as it was tasted. First Karl, then Mick, their faces opening into a wash of pleasure. Davey sniffed suspiciously at the bowl and shook his head, declaring it too green.

'Here.' Frenchie topped my egg with a small mound of the paste. 'Taste.' He waved the spoon at me accusingly. 'Food is joy. To make. To eat.' I couldn't tell if his eyes were wet from the temperature, from the ocean, or from emotion. He glanced at my boiled egg. 'This is not dinner. This is not joy.'

'It is to me.' I swallowed, the yolk slipping down my throat.

Raising his level of insult, still pointing towards my egg, the engineer added, 'Only the English eat like this. And Americans.'

'Jesus, Frenchie. Give the girl a fricking break.'

'It's no break, skipper.' Green drops splattered from his spoon as he waved it. 'It is just truth.' He pronounced *is* as *eez*, so that he sounded like that cartoon skunk Pepé Le Pew, which was the closest I'd come to knowing a Frenchman before now.

Mick wiped at his beard, said, 'He was like this with the last cook.' He glared at Frenchie. 'And look how well that worked out.'

'What, um, what happened to the last crew, then?' Karl smeared a piece of white sliced bread with Frenchie's green paste and folded it in two. His plate was still half full of my meat delight.

Frenchie became suddenly busy with his cutlery, polishing it on a piece of paper towel, scrubbing intensely, holding the knife blade up to his reflection. We sat, waiting, Davey wiping the last of the flavourless meat from his plate with more bread, Karl with his head tilted to the side. He asked again, 'What happened? I mean, you lost the lot of them.'

Silence pattered about the galley, only filtered by the buzzing of the fluoro light. Finally, the skipper said, 'Cook and mate decided to go off to WA. Decky decided fishing wasn't for him. Right, crew – ' he slapped his hands on to the table, one loud beat ' – time to shoot away. Let's go.'

I had no idea what shooting meant, but I followed them out onto the deck, into the dripping sunset.

Miss Pitt was my secondary school English teacher. Long-legged, with a boy's haircut, she paced the length of the classroom, pointing, calling, demanding. When I finished school, she took me aside, said, 'Kacey, you have all the potential in the world. Don't waste it. Please don't.' But by then she'd disappointed me by marrying a man, growing her hair into a blonde bob for the wedding and turning into Mrs Him after it. Before she disappeared herself into someone else's name, she introduced me to Slessor, to Hopkins, to the pleasures of speaking poetry aloud, to the thrill of the word. At night, I sat in the scrappy shed with the mosquitoes buzzing on my skin and I made my own heart pound by chanting poems, feeling myself taken elsewhere, any elsewhere, anywhere but there in that dank and dark shed. I had not yet read Larkin, not come across his explanation that when removed from the familiar, you are perceived differently, and so you perceive yourself differently. But even then, I knew the possibilities of elsewhere, knew that if I got there, I could be different too. And now, orange disc crashing down, seabirds skreaking and skerrecking, there I was: elsewhere. Better than the open road, I had the open sea. Hopkins: that was what I thought of then. His dappled vermilion gold burning ember birds, his thick painted world that had creaked my body and my longing open. At the stern of the boat, I stretched my arms out, turned my face to the horizon. Sleek wavelets crimped around us, coated in red, in gold, so solid, so real that I felt myself to be in a painting or a poem. Seabirds swooped and scooped on the shining surface of the sea, and there was nothing – no land, no boundary – to be seen. Just the *Ocean Thief* and the round circle of orange sun sitting fat on the horizon and yes, I thought, yes. This is the story, the song, that I have been waiting for, the one that is better than me.

Karl shouted behind me, an instruction, and I tried to shake myself awake, to remember that I was here to work, though I had no idea what that work would look like.

'Get the nets.' Karl grabbed at my arm, pointed me back towards the galley. 'You and Davey can take starboard – when I call, shoot the nets out – use the rope, here. I'll winch them down, you need to make sure nothing catches, yeah? Keep the nets clear.' He pointed to the end of the boom. 'We want them out, so they can go wide. And the boards – see here? – they need to open when they drop in, to keep the weight on. Got it? Let's go.'

I didn't have it; everything he said had rushed over me while I nodded in a panic and tried to make the words attach to some object. Nets, I could see. Boards? Winch? How badly wrong could it go?

Karl raised his hand, nodded up to the skipper, and the grunt of the engine escalated, along with a new sound, the roar of the winch. Nets swayed over the aluminium tray, with orange ropes tied at the ends, and while Karl shouted instructions, Davey and I yanked at the ropes, threw them out over the gunwale and shoved at them as the nets dropped in, each of us watching the other, nervy as unbroken horses. Water and sky merged, folding about us, and the ropes slipped into the water like snakes. They lay flat and hungry, until the weight of the boards and the thrust of the boat combined to swallow them, disappearing like a gulp of food. The whole thing: the rise of excitement, the sudden rush, the dance of the nets on the water, the swallowing of the sea, it all made a light ripple through me. It was the ripple of possibility, and of beauty. I was here, living it, being it. Fuck being on the road, being a cipher or a muse for the boys' own adventure: I was on the sea, and I was alive, as alive as I could ever hope to be.

DARKNESS CAME QUICKLY. Traces of orange fire spread like oil across the water behind the boat, making a widening lane in our wake. Nameless birds flipped and soared, dipping into the disappearing light, and below them one fin, then another, and another, arcing in perfect rhythm.

'It never gets old.' Karl squeezed my arm, pointing to the dolphins leaping and dipping alongside the *Ocean Thief*.

The light was going but I could still make out the ash-grey slick of dolphin skin, the squint of their small eyes, the curve of their beaks looking so much like smirking smiles. A calf leaped into the air beside its mother and, like a child, I squealed and clapped my hands, called for more. I could barely believe that I deserved this, watching these beauties while the last of the sun left reflections on their backs. I was as far away as I could be, as far away as I'd hoped to be. I was not that child in the bunk bed wondering how to escape; I had escaped, I was almost free, I would be free.

We waited until the dolphins dropped back, or beneath, and then Karl said, 'Come on, I'll help you clean the galley. Only tonight. Only once.'

Inside, Frenchie was parked at the table, his round belly prodding the table, a pack of cards laid out before him in an intense game of solitaire. Dirty plates toppled on the lip of the baize cloth. Reddish sauce trailed from the side of the table.

'Here.' Davey's arm, skinny and pale, reached across the table, his grubby nails flicking under one of the glossy cards. 'The black five on the six.'

'Jesus. That is no good, no good at all.' The engineer's hand slapped down on Davey's. 'You don't interrupt a person's game.' The rims of his eyes were red, his fingertips a deep yellow.

Although he was older than Karl – older than me, too – Davey had the air of a child, and the soft unformed muscles of one. The milkiness of his arms in those first days was a source of wonder to me. Later, he said he'd spent the last months working inside a factory, slapping stickers onto plastic boxes. He laughed, said, 'Challenging work for the likes of me,' and for the first time I thought that maybe he was smart, smarter than I'd imagined. He was one of those kids who couldn't sit still, couldn't find a home at school, with the desks and boards and boredom, but despite that could be happy anywhere; just a living, that was all he wanted. Some money to go back home to Queensland and pay some rent and live near his mum. It was a mystery to me: the only place I'd ever found home was among books and words and learning, there in the rustle of pages where I could disappear, where I could *think*. That was where I had meaning, though it came with the cost of wanting more than I had. Davey needed none of that. Only to live, only to *be*. That was enough.

The flabby smell of beef filled the galley, swelling on the scent of diesel, and I scrubbed at the pans, trying to hold my breath until I could be outside again, with the air and the sea and the dolphins.

Footsteps clomped on the ladder that led from the galley to the wheelhouse and the laughter around the table settled as though the teacher was on their way. He didn't come all the way down, as though unsure of his welcome. He spoke to me, and to Davey, doubled in half, squinting down, trying to look friendly, like one of the gang. He said, 'You'd better get some sleep. We'll likely pull up about one.'

'One in the morning?'

'Yup. Get some sleep. And you – ' he nodded at Frenchie ' – be on your best.'

I waited till he climbed back up to the wheelhouse before I slid onto the bench beside Frenchie. 'What does he mean, be on your best?'

'Nothing. I don't know. He's – nothing. Perhaps it is because usually the skipper has the cook and you are not his.' He moved a glossy jack of spades, placed it on a red queen.

'Sorry, what? I'm not his; I'm not anyone's.' But I could feel my throat tightening.

Karl's curls shimmered about his face. 'Nope. I told you I'd keep my eye out. That's not happening. He needs me more than he needs you. Anyway, he's made it a dry boat, he's okay. He wants a decent catch more than he wants a quick fuck.'

'I can hear you.' The feet were just above us, Mick's bearded face smiling down at us. 'At least wait until I'm out of earshot. One: ask Frenchie why it's a dry boat. Two: I'm married. Happily. Or I will be as soon as I get back. Three: we're here to work. Which is how I'm going to pay for the wedding. And the house. Four: get some sleep.'

And then he was gone again, but the wake behind him was lighter, easier, and I was grateful for his interjection.

But we didn't sleep. Instead we sat at the table moving Frenchie's cards around until he snatched them away, told us in his thick accent to bloody off. When Karl asked to bloody-what-off – Bugger off? Fuck off? Get off? – Frenchie gathered all the cards in, his arms sweeping across the table. 'Just bloody off,' he said. 'That's all. Bloody.'

The cards reflected the stark white light as he bound them with a green rubber band and tucked them into the groove between the table and wall. Karl made another pot of coffee then we told story after story of our lives. Davey told us about his first job, washing dishes in a bistro, and how the owner kept slipping his hand into his pocket and jiggling while he watched the girls bending over the low sink, and he told us about his mother's homemade mint slice, and I told them about Sylvie going off to India and how I'd almost gone too but changed my mind at the last minute, just before we booked the tickets, and then I told them about how I'd had a boyfriend in a band in the city, a bass player, and who knew what would happen with us when I got back, if I ever went back.

Was it Frenchie or Karl who told the story of the machete? I'm pretty sure it was Frenchie, but later, when I came to claim some of those stories for my own, their origins got murky.

Hours passed; we made toast, and drank more coffee, and made each other laugh and roll our eyes, and then Frenchie said, 'Before this boat I was on the *Pearl*.' To Karl, he said, 'You know the *Pearl*?'

Karl shook his head. 'Which fleet?'

There were scores of boats in the gulf at that time. Their lights dotted the water, flicking on and off, homely beacons. Beneath the surface of the water, the ocean was being stripped: net after net hauled to decks of boat after boat. The *Pearl* was just one of those boats from one of those fleets. And on that boat, Frenchie had his first engineer's job in Australia. The skipper was a drunkard, beginning with a morning beer and moving to bourbon by the afternoon, throwing the bottles overboard when they were empty so that the crew could never keep track. Not that it mattered; they were all weaving and bobbing about the *Pearl*, not one of them ever quite sober.

One night the skipper drank his second bottle of bourbon and was barely able to keep them on course. The first mate – a bloke from Far North Queensland who never showered and stank like the mud from the flats – took charge, got the nets in, kept them on course, until the skipper got his bloody back up and stomped up to the wheelhouse. Bloody mate taking over. Trying to get the girl. Always the trouble was the girl. Skipper shouted so loud spit was coming out of his mouth; what the bloody hell was the mate doing driving the boat? Was he the skipper? And still the *Pearl* motored up and down the trench line, the nets dragging behind.

The girl was English. Blonde. Going around all the time in a bikini top and little shorts. Already sleeping with the skipper. Almost definitely. Probably, anyway. And while the shouting and spitting is going on, she's in her cabin with the door locked. She doesn't want to know. Causing the trouble and then getting out of the way.

Frenchie shrugged at this point, the reds of his eyes showing.

And then, out on the gulf, there is the loud horn of another trawler. The *Pearl* has drifted over, off her path, almost smashing into another boat. The mate signals the other crew, gets them out of the way. Everything is good. All calm. But then there's the skipper, pissed as a bird, and he's waving a huge curved machete over his head, threatening to kill the mate, weaving his way around the deck, and it's all looking pretty bad. Cook is screaming in her cabin, decky hiding out in the galley.

Frenchie has to do something – someone has to, anyway – and so he clambers down to the chug and comfort of the engine room, where the heat blossoms up with the roar of the motor and wraps him in certainty before he kills the power, all of it. Lights. Motor. Action. He's locked the door to the engine room and no one else can get down there, no one can work the power, it is all his, Frenchie's, down there in the hot dark.

The *Pearl* drifts, dark and invisible, on the current. The screaming from the cabin stops. The machete drops with a clunk to the deck. The skipper shouts, *What the fuck? What did you do, engineer?* But Frenchie is in the dark womb of his engine room, humming to himself, and if they nudge another trawler, or drift too far, he cannot be to blame. He waits there, as though it is a bunker, for the fire to stop. With the earphones on his ears, warm like a hug, and the air like a smelter around him, he dozes off, his chin falling to his chest, his back against the soft folding deckchair he has down there. The skipper cannot bring lights on, even the navigation lights are off; nothing is what he can do; not switch on an engine, nothing.

In the morning, Frenchie climbs up to the deck, grainy-mouthed, to find the cook sitting in the wheelhouse with the machete across her knees and a marine patrol boat heading towards them. She keeps the machete on her knees, nods at Frenchie, says, 'The others have passed out. I radioed in. The lead boat is coming out to collect us. It's over.'

She didn't even say sorry. She didn't even say thank you.

And that is why Frenchie is on this boat, the *Ocean Thief*, with a green crew – yes, okay, except for the mate, who is not green, certainly – and a cook who can't make food taste good and who thinks an egg in a cup is dinner. Like a bloody English.

I FELT THE CHANGE in the engine before I heard it – a deeper thrust, a twist, something exciting building. And then the shift in gearing; a horn sounding and Karl pounding on my door, his gleeful voice calling that it was time, that we were up. On the deck, everything felt charged: the swoop and cry of the seabirds, the furrowing excitement of the arcing and zigzagging fins, the deeper dark of the sky. Karl was a kinetic dash, leaping from the upper deck to the high trays, looping down to the bottom deck, throwing ropes to Davey, to me, and to the unwilling engineer. Roll-up drooping from his lips, Frenchie curved into an upright comma, an unwilling pause on deck.

Behind the galley door, four striped butcher's aprons hung, splattered with green and grey. Below them, neatly laid out like shoes in a children's story, four pairs of gumboots. Karl handed me an apron; it drooped down to my shins; I tied a knot at the neck, marking it as mine.

'I don't need the boots. I'm a barefoot girl.'

'You need to wear them for this. There's all sorts of shit that comes out of the sea and we need a working crew.'

I slid my feet into the boots, toes curling at the damp, slightly sticky insides.

He handed me a pair of thick plastic gloves, the colour of raspberry cordial. 'You'll need these too.'

In the wheelhouse on the top deck, the skipper slipped the engine into reverse to make us slow and stop. Despite the slowing of the hulk of the *Ocean Thief*, everything else escalated: Karl leaping and shouting, the birds squawking, the sharks slipping closer. Everything around us could feel the change as the nets closed and drew to the surface. Karl held his arm up as he winched, calling for us to wait, to hold, to be ready. I had no idea what was happening, or how, but everything in my body was charged, on high alert, and I was soaring like the birds making circles at the stern of the boat.

It was like a reverse birth when it happened: the mouth of the net and then of the water closing, a suspension while the winch connected to the straining nets. And then, on either side of the boat, an ascension of two nets, made sack-shaped with the life within them, the crush of shining scales, the shine of eyes. Karl heaved at the winch, and up the nets came, over and across. He called to me and Davey, and we tugged at the ropes, heaving the nets across to the midpoint of the boat, and while the skipper shouted at us to move it, to work faster, to shift our arses, we untied the nets and the mouths opened. Karl was whooping, arms raised in victory, but I watched the tumble of faces, of beings, of beauty, and my bubble blistered, festered, seeping something poisonous into me like pus.

Everything had slowed as the nets lifted, but then it turned, escalating into a frenzy of noise and speed and action. The catch tumbled to the tray, thousands of fish, scores of species, all caught up with weed and clump and cockle shells. I tried to feel nothing, to be hard, but I watched a cod the size of my own body, its cartoonish lips fat and curved into a serious frown; I knew I was holding everything up, but the cod was brown and speckled grey, its wide eyes bulging right at me and *I must not anthropomorphise, I must not anthropomorphise*, but I swear it gazed right at me, right into me, with fear or desperation or the hope for help. Did cod feel hope? Desperation, surely. *I must not anthropomorphise.* But was the capacity to *feel* solely human? Then solely which sort of human? Those boys with their cars and their laughter and their door-locking, bra-flicking, dick-flashing; those boys, I must assume, believed my feelings to be different from, or less than, theirs. The cod's mouth opened, lips back, tail flipping.

'Kacey! Get on it!' Mick hollered from the upper deck and he was right: this was not the time to be gazing dully at a dying fish. Still, I called back over my shoulder, to Davey, to Frenchie, to anyone who would listen, calling for help to lift and heave the cod back to the sea. They both helped, grunting with the weight of it, and we shuffled to the portside and dropped it in. Water fountained up around it; a shudder on the surface, and then it was gone, dropping down as quickly as rain.

Karl shouted something at me, gesturing towards a heavy hose, and I swung it into the tray while he blasted the water in. A small shark flipped beneath me, and I picked it up by the tail, ran to the gunwale, and heaved it out, dropping it into the water. We didn't want sharks. We didn't want cod, or this beautiful rainbow-scaled fish looking me right in the eye, its gills contracting in the wrong air, its lips puckering. We wanted the curved green prawns that scrabbled in the middle of the catch.

I didn't expect it to be so industrial-loud. I didn't expect the metal trays, and the chutes washing the life down, letting us sift and sort and throw, until the chutes expelled what was left back to the ocean. For a while, I tried to extract the larger creatures: the bream, the trevally, the sailfish. At first, I saw them, the large flailing fish, and I slipped my hands under the wet scales, the slippery slide of them, and I threw them into the sea, then ran back to the chute. Legs straddled against the rocking deck, we positioned ourselves on either side of the tray. At first, I reached and threw, reached and threw. Reached for the spiky green tail of a green prawn and tossed it to the chute, threw a reef shark, a bream, a coral trout back to the ocean. But I couldn't keep up, I couldn't rescue the undeserving fish, couldn't throw enough of them back, and they kept coming, shooting down in streams. My gloved hands seemed disconnected from the rest of my body; bright red in the gloves, rapidly moving, thoughtless. Karl grinned at me from the other side of the chute and shouted, 'Catch more money!' and I remembered then why I was there, where it would lead me. My hands moved faster, grabbing for the tentacles or tails, the green sharp against the silver and grey and white. I saw only the throng, the heaving pile of scale and spike and skin as an amorphous whole, a spongy mass. Fish dropped down past me, no longer gasping for air, and in the higher ends of the tray the larger fish thrashed only lightly in the low water.

Something red flashed near me on the tray and Frenchie yelped. Gleeful, child-like, he bolted past me, shouting at Karl to hold off on washing the catch down the tray. Striped apron slapping at his knees, roll-up still drooping from his mouth, he heaved himself up to the tray until he stood in the metal sea of dying fish. His knees looked bony above the wide lip of his gumboots.

'What the fuck, Frenchie?' Mick's hands were clean, but above us, from the upper deck, he saw everything, like God.

Frenchie was doubled over, elbows wide. When he stood again, he was holding a reddish fish in both arms, cradling it like a baby, and shouting. Karl shouted back; above the wash on the trays and the engine I couldn't hear the words until the wash of water stopped.

'Red emperor. Red emperor for dinner. And bugs.' For the first time, Frenchie was grinning, prancing on the deck in his clumpy boots and grimy apron. Under Frenchie's instruction,

Davey filled one of the trench-like buckets with extra water, and Frenchie dropped the gleaming fish into it.

I couldn't bear to look at it, but when I went back to the chute my hands began moving again, but not fast enough, not precise enough. The catch shot down, faster, and I stopped noticing, stopped connecting with the gills, with the lips, with the creatures thrashing without water. I no longer paused to deliver fish back to the ocean, no longer held the catch up so that I could save one creature from the slow suffocation of breathing air when it should be in water. Now, I reached, flicked, threw; it was a game, only a game. My hands, red, shining, grabbed prawns and threw them to the side chutes. The speed became numbing, the endless sweep of scale and skin indifferent. *Catch more money. Catch more money.* I reached, sorted, threw, racing against myself and against the nauseating swell rising in my stomach until the rush of fish and crustaceans slowed.

And then it was over.

The lower deck made me think of the aftershock of a children's party, with streamers scattered across tables, crisps and chocolates trodden underfoot, torn crêpe paper banners. Instead of chocolate trodden underfoot, it was small fish. Trails of skin and weed were strewn across the stern, tiny white fish – sand whiting perhaps – flipped about the deck; scattered across the tray not streamers but lengths of knobbly weed and seagrass. It was as though we'd spent the last hour in a frenzied food fight, throwing fish and grass and water at each other while music pounded.

The frenzy and the greed were gone, and now it was just the shabby remnants. We hosed and swept and washed; we rinsed the nets and tied them neatly above the tray; we coiled ropes and we watched the sharks slowly drifting behind us. We laid the catch out in white cardboard boxes, weighing and counting. Karl checked and rechecked, shaking his head. And finally, when the deck was empty and the sharks had disappeared and there was once more just the twinkling gold of the fleets of trawlers across the water, then we peeled off our gloves, stepped out of the slimy boots and fell into our respective cabins.

Lying in the cabin, my body shook slightly, the lack of sleep burning in my veins like a drug. Fibreglass shards brushed against my hand inside the bunk. The colour of fibreglass, the mottled tan of the underside, the fibres threading through it, even the chemical smell – they made me think of flesh. Of the inside of a brain, of something troubling, something almost dead but once alive.

This was where I could be safe. Here, surrounded by strangers; here in this almost dead bunk, here in the dark. Beneath me, the engine thrummed, cradling me. Humming like a song; warming me, too. Lying there, I wished again, more than before, that I'd been born different, or elsewhere, or to someone else. Anything but what I had. Anything but me.

I hadn't known, hadn't anticipated, the way my body would shake with work, would unravel with exhaustion. I didn't anticipate, didn't know, that this unravelling would come with a stirring up of the past, a tearing up of memory. While we churned the depth of the gulf, my carefully buried memories churned and swam up. I'd been dancing, shouting over the sound of my own story. On the *Ocean Thief*, with such a narrow field of distraction, everything that I'd been shouting over – all the din, all the churning mud – came swimming up. And I was not ready.

Darkness then. The muffle of sleep. Spit drying on my lips, the depths of sleep so dreamless, exhaustion carrying it down. What a pleasure it is, that sudden and seamless descent, the going under, the giving over, the annihilation of the self.

THERE IS A TIME before the word, before understanding how the word could give shape, give power, give reason. There is only jumbled confusion: the shape of him, his large booming voice; the tucked-away shape of her, the wetness of being swallowed by her. There is another shape then – or, rather, the absence of a shape. It is merely sound: my sister crying, a key turning in a lock, footsteps walking away, another door closing. The sound of my mother going away to rest.

This is before language, before words. So even these things – shape, sound, swallow – they are inventions. I have only the feeling, made formless without language. Without language, what I know is this: those feelings are too big for me. They will swallow me up and destroy me. I will be annihilated.

Annihilated is a word I learn later. Aunty June, who is not my aunty, is looking after me. Sally is her daughter and I love Sally more than I love any other person. And I want to be in their family. Aunty June irons clothes in the middle of the day, the sweet smell of Fabulon and water steaming the air while the television murmurs. There are people kissing on the television, and then a lady slaps a man and cries; I am very quiet because I know that Aunty June has forgotten I am here and, if she sees me, she won't let me watch the kissing. The kissing makes me feel crumbly in my pants. At the start of the show there is an hourglass, like the egg timer on Aunty June's stovetop, and sand goes through it and the man you can't see but can only hear says that the sand is like the days of our lives.

In the corner of Aunty June's lounge room, I arrange my Fuzzy Felt – giraffe kissing elephant, lion putting his mouth on lady lion – and think about the days of our lives and the hourglass and then I think about it some more. When the programme ends and there is another programme, but still with people slapping and kissing and crying, I think about it some more. And I still don't understand how sand or glass is like me, like my days. I count on my hand how many years I am – three – and I think that when I start kindy and I am four, I will ask the teacher. The teacher will know everything, and she will tell me all the things.

It's on the hourglass show that *annihilated* happens. Aunty June turns over one of Uncle Doug's shirts, sprinkling water on it from the pale yellow Tupperware cup. Crispness creases the air and a small puff of steam rises. Something happens on the screen in the corner and Aunty June puts the iron down on the ironing board, turns her face towards the screen. Something good is happening, something that might give me the crumblypants feeling again, and so I go very quiet, very invisible, the way I have taught myself, and I watch the people inside the television box. They are not kissing but shouting and the man puts his hands on the lady's shoulders, and he shouts right in her face: *I will annihilate you.* And then he kisses her against the wall, and she kisses him right back.

Annihilate. I turn it over and over in my mouth, whispering it so quietly that Aunty June thinks I am singing or mumbling. She doesn't know all the thoughts and all the words I am storing up. I store them up to save me. Annihilate.

Later I take a crayon and I think about the word. I have a sheet of butcher's paper from Firth's Butchers on the corner of Fourth

Street, and it is spread right across the back porch of Aunty June's house. The sound of the word is so sure, and I make it there on the butcher's paper, in green crayon and in ugly purple, the ugliest of all the colours. Right across the paper it goes, tearing the corners with its sharpness and then I walk on the paper, walk right there on the word, stomping around it and over it. When Sally comes home from kindy, I will tell her what I have learned because she is not the only one who gets to learn things. Here on the back porch of her house words are being made, and it's almost as good as school.

The screen door squeaks and then crashes. Round hinges keep it open sometimes and then when it closes it makes the sound of a thunder-clap. Aunty June has a peanut butter sandwich for me, on a yellow plastic plate. She walks around the word carefully and then she says, 'We'll fold up your picture now,' and she gathers up the paper and puts it away.

'It's not a picture,' I say. 'It's writing.'

And this is the only time I hate Aunty June, when she laughs and says, 'Writing? Words?' As if there is something funny and not terrifying about my ugly purple on the butcher's paper. When my mother comes to collect me at the end of the day the two of them stand on the back step talking quietly and I hear Aunty June say to my mother, 'Funny little thing, isn't she? Scribble all over the place, but she's convinced she's writing words.' My mother laughs too. Annihilate.

I can hear them that night. I can hear her saying, Please, Joe, no, Joe, please, and I can hear him with his shouting, and I can hear the thumping against the wall, the wetness of her, the crying of her, and I blanket myself with words. Tucking myself under them, the warmth of them, I think of my hand holding not a crayon but a pencil, making mark after mark on the page, and they will be words and people – all the grown-ups even

– will hear them and see them. In the room next door there is just weepy breathing and him being the worst kind of quiet, too quiet. My hand holding the pencil; I can see it. Curving the letters one after the other and the letters make words and the words can pile up one after the other and they can be warm, and they can make a wall.

There are other things we don't say. Words that stay beneath us and, if they are spoken, we let them fall to the ground and we look away, pretend that we have not seen or heard. Uncle Doug is a drunk. The painter is ugly. My father has a mistress.

Outside, later, the moon is low over the Sweeneys' roof at the end of the street and I've woken from the dream of flying, swimming through the air like a puppy or a princess. Something has woken me, a loud wail, getting louder, the sound of her in the dining room outside my door, crying onto the table. Moon still pulsing, I fly myself down from above Boolaroo, down from above the upturned faces of my sisters watching, mouths open. Now I am here, on my bunk, listening to her crying outside. She gets louder and louder. It is not necessary for her to say the words, Come out here and pat me like a puppy or a princess. I know that this is what the words in the air, the ones not spoken, are saying. I stand beside her, patting her on the back, waiting for her to stop crying and to say, I saw you flying. Or: Time for sleep. Anything. But instead of that she cries and cries and cries and, 'Thank you,' she says, 'for making me feel better. Stay here for a minute and cuddle me some more.'

I pat her back and feel myself disappearing into the well of her sadness. I think of the words, of all the things I can name, the steps that will make a ladder to get me out of here. I think about *moon* and I think about *bait*, the word I saw on the side of the new fish-and-chip shop in Speers Point. *Ba-it*. I can make the sounds in my head, I can understand the letters now, but I can't understand the word, and there is too much sadness and noise around to ask. *Bait*, I think. *Moon*. And I pat her back, whispering the words, making a ladder to climb me out of the well.

BEFORE DAWN, there was the pounding again on my door, and a repeat of the net rising, pulling in, sorting and washing. On deck, the red emperor gazed up blankly from the plastic trench and I looked away, at the tray, at the tip of the trawling booms, anywhere else. Once more we hauled up a fat, full net; once more I looked away from the mass of glazed eyes; once more I threw small sharks to the sea, and once more I sifted prawns in a frenzy, until I couldn't see the individual creatures flipping and gasping on the tray. In the middle of the rush I saw only a mass, nameless, shapeless, and a job I had to do. Straining at the winch, hauling up the net, I saw only the thing I needed: money. Once more the tray emptied, leaving only fleshy remnants. Red light, then gold, washed over the gulf, and then over the *Ocean Thief* as the sorting came to an end. At the bow, a pod of dolphins surfed, squeaking and flipping, the low sun glinting off their backs. Karl scratched numbers into the columns in the black book, shaking his head again, then swung to the upper deck in two moves. Below him, I hosed out the tray, slapping at the last tendrils while Karl and the skipper stood on the upper deck, huddling together, arms folded, looking at the wide horizon.

Between the open deck and the enclosed space of the galley and the cabins, a canopy covered a series of metal benches and sinks. There, we left our boots and aprons, and there, we boxed up the catch while Karl blasted music across the deck. Always music with gravelly men singing about their needs and their wants, or about long road journeys where they're going to get their girl. So loud that we had to shout across it; so loud that even the seabirds fluttered away. Like hell's antechamber, or heaven's, depending on what time of day you walked through it.

I was tugging my boots off under the canopy, ready to sleep again, when Karl hissed in my ear, 'Breakfast.'

I nodded. 'I'll put some toast on.'

'For real, Kacey? We need food. Real food. Eggs. Sausages.'

Nausea rose in my mouth at the thought of pink sausage flesh, the spots of mince escaping into pimples on the skin; the stink of the meat, the way it would fill the small galley. I nodded miserably and began grabbing eggs from the industrial-sized fridge. On the bottom shelf I found a tub of pink sausages and some watery-looking tomatoes, and I moved things around in the family-sized frying pan until it seemed like a meal, like something that the fisherman in a John West-the-Best commercial would eat.

The skipper dropped the anchor, and after the rattling grind of the anchor chain there was the sudden shock of silence. Engine off. Chain stilled. The bass and rattling guitars of Cold Chisel hushed. A brief murmur from the wheelhouse where Karl and Mick were laying out routes and charts, and then, nothing. Like a blanket being dropped over us; perfect stillness, perfect quiet.

We ate, leaving scrapes of sauce and sausage fat and tomato flesh spread across plates and the sticky baize tablecloth and finally, finally, finally, the galley was empty. There was at last just me, and there was quiet. For a moment, at least. Suds bubbled warmly on my wrists while I scraped and rubbed at the thick white dishes. I thought about my mother, about trips she did with Neil – and before that, with my father – when the men would do the driving, and the planning, and the tinkering with engines or maps or rudders, and the ladies – my mother and whichever wife was accompanying her – did the cooking and wrapping and thinking about food. Sometimes they arranged boat trips, motoring out to the scabby sand island in the middle of Lake Macquarie in my stepfather's little half-cabin. The men would stand by the shore discussing maps and routes, traffic, the best use of boat ramps and winch power. The women huddled around eskies and rugs, discussing recipes and food: the preparing, the eating and the withholding of food. Voices sharply bright, ready to turn to a spiky snap, they listed ingredients and then patted at their own thighs, tutting. The men looked at the outside world, at how to navigate it, and the women looked at the body. How to nurture it, how to feed it, how to control it. Annoyance simmered in me, the way it did in those women.

Outside, I washed the deck alongside Davey, then climbed onto the tray while Karl showed me how to check the nets, lifting, stretching, dropping. They were heavier than I expected, the weight pleasing. Balanced on the brink of the high tray, arms raised above me, I squinted up at the net.

Frenchie tapped on my feet. 'Cook.' It wasn't a command but a salutation.

Fuck off, I thought. Cook is not my name and it's not the job I want. He tapped again, his nails scraping on my ankle bone. I kicked his hand away.

He tapped again. 'Kacey. Come with me.'

On the other side of the tray, his arms heaped with netting, Davey said, 'Go. I'll lay these out.'

Frenchie took me by the arm, led me as though I were a pet or a horse to the long trench-like bucket, the glossy red emperor lying glazed in the small space, the eyes bulging. The engineer said, 'I kill him. You cook him.'

I must have looked blank. Or repulsed. I must have shown something on my face, because Frenchie pulled me closer to the fish, bobbed down to it so that we were both squatting alongside the tray. 'Here – ' Frenchie pointed to the spine of the fish ' – you will slice him. Lemons. Capers. Butter.' He took a knife from his belt; sun glinted off the blade and – I couldn't tell; was it a machete? Was it stained with oil or blood? Was it him, Frenchie, with his red eyes and yellow nails, who had circled the deck waving the machete on the *Pearl*? Was it him, after all, who threatened the mate, the decky, the girl?

He raised the knife – the machete, I suppose – and sliced it down in a fast swoop, hitting a spot below the emperor's gills. Pink scales quivered as the fish, glorious, gazing, twitched. Its mouth opened slightly. Blood trickled from the wound, swirling in the water. Frenchie squatted by the bucket, dabbing at the scales of the dying creature. 'Good,' he said. 'This will be delicious. So now – ' he turned back to me ' – we take him inside, I show you how to fillet him, and you cook him. Tonight, with bugs. This is the feast of the sea. It is why we are here.'

The eye of the fish began to turn cloudy. I said, 'I'm not cutting that fish and I'm not eating it. You can fillet it and I'll put it in the oven.' One fish, only one shining creature, and I stared at it, watching life leach from it.

Frenchie peered at me. 'You are sentimental. Just sentimental. They are here for us, for our use. That's what they are for.'

I stared at him for a moment, wondering whose use I was for.

Frenchie cradled the fish – the size of a baby, a human one – and carried it into the galley. He said, 'I do not wish to work on the deck today. Today, I will cook this feast. You do my work on the deck for me.' He tied a half-apron about his waist and squatted down in front of the fridge, muttering to himself, then glanced up at me. 'Go. I wish to be here.'

Outside, I coiled the ropes and Karl showed me how to check the cable on the winch, how to sidle out to the trawling boom and test the chains that held the boards. Rust scratched into the soles of my bare feet, the heat scorching me, but when I hitched my arm over the upper beam and heaved at the chains, I was a warrior. Standing on the narrow beam with the silvery ocean glinting beneath me, I told myself that I was brave, as strong as a boy, as a man, as anyone.

Later, we dropped the nets again as the sun set and the water began to boil. In the galley, Frenchie bustled – the red apron knotted about his waist, an array of knives and boards spread out on the thin bench. He was bright with pleasure, flicking scales away from the pink of the fish, pressing garlic cloves and whipping the skin away with one thumbnail. Awkwardly, uselessly, I offered to cook potatoes, and he glanced at me briefly, then shook his head. 'I am happy here, and you – ' he nodded towards the deck ' – you are happy there.'

Such a simple thing, to be seen, to have your own desires seen; such a simple thing, such simple pleasure.

Davey and I stood out on deck, faces to the wind, until the last of the light left. Frenchie called us in to the galley, presented a tray of fish baked with herbs and butter and sweet carrots. Instead of the diesel smell of beef, the air was rich with something golden and sweet, an overlay of garlic. The baize cloth was covered with dishes: creamy potatoes, broccoli and almonds, Moreton Bay bugs in a deep tomato stew. He was like a proud parent, bustling and pointing, demanding that we taste, notice, enjoy, and even Davey – wary of garlic, and of almonds, and of broccoli – piled a plate high, swallowing in a blissed silence.

Frenchie squeezed beside me, so close that the hairs on his arm bristled on my skin. He said, 'You taste the fish. This is food. Real food. Taste.'

'I told you, I'm not eating it. I watched it die. I don't want to eat it.'

He slapped his hand on the table. 'This is beautiful. This is for us.' A tear dripped onto his long nose. 'Why are you on a fishing boat, if you won't eat this food? Why?'

The table was silent then, Karl, Mick, Davey all watching the engineer squinting at me, his hand still on the table, his face wet while he waited for my answer. The scraping of plates, the chewing and swallowing, all was suspended while they waited.

I moved some potatoes around on my plate and kept my eyes on my fork. I said, 'I had nowhere else to go.'

A pause while they each looked at each other, uncertain. And then Karl laughed. 'Me too. That's everyone in the gulf. Who else would have us?'

After we ate, Frenchie said, 'From now on, I cook. You do my deck work. Yes?'

Yes, I said, yes.

'I do only this and the engine room.'

'Okay.'

'But you clean up the dishes.'

'Yes.'

Later still, when the galley was empty and the last of the grease washed away, he added, 'Kacey, you watch my back. I cover you, I cook, and you cover me. You watch my back for me.'

Yes, I said again, of course yes, though I didn't know – couldn't know – what it might mean, to cover his back, to risk my own.

BENEATH ME the churn of the engine was warm and soft, a soothing purr that lulled me. Already, time had become watery and I struggled to count the days I'd been on board. Lemony light beamed across my legs, angled up to make a resting place for my book. *Lives of Girls and Women.* I found it in the book exchange store in the Smith Street Mall in Darwin. I chose it for the cover – a headless man with a green field behind him – and for the glossy new smell of the pages. In front of me, the lines blurred, the yellow light flashing into shadow, the words tumbling. I thought about the story Frenchie told on my first night on the boat, of the cook and the engineer and the machete. I wondered how it might feel to hold a machete, to swing it. How it might feel, for instance, to find the barrister with the spot on his nose and the pointed chin, and to hold the machete up to his face, the gleam bouncing off it while I smiled. It was the barrister I wanted to find, or the horse-faced cop, more than the taxi driver. I didn't know the driver's name, I will never know his name, and later, when I try to find the records of my case, that will strike the records folk in the Office of Public Prosecutions as odd. Why would I not know his name? Why would I not notice, recall, attend? Why would a girl disconnect in that way?

If I was innocent, I would remember. If I was innocent, if I'd been a good girl.

Fury

The pages of *Lives of Girls and Women* were rough – a poor-quality print-run with some repeated pages. My thumb rubbed against a corner. I thought about the weight of the machete, about a headless man. Swing, flick, slice. Like Supergirl. Forgetting, pretending to forget, that I couldn't even use my beautiful golden flick knife, not when it came to it. Outside, the water swirled while our nets trailed on the bottom of the seabed. Earlier, the surface had been calm and solid, glassy smooth. Now, all that perfect settled silt would be churned up, turned up, torn up. A mess would be made. I was being undone. I could feel it, could feel my tight hold on myself loosening, unravelling. Like the net, I was unbound, muddy memories emerging unbidden and unwelcome, the weight of me dropping, ready to be sorted.

Half dozing, I felt the machete in my hands, the whip of it through the air, and it was Ben Billman I swung it at; Ben Billman, the red-faced next-door neighbour with his fat hands and his stumpy legs; Ben Billman, who owned the rented house that we lived in; Ben Billman, with the caravan in his backyard and the family of kittens and the oblivious wife. Ben fucking Billman. Silt should sometimes settle but now, with the engine shifting into a grunt beneath me, it churned up, the remembering and the rage and, when I finally told, the chorus of voices asking, 'Why didn't you say anything? Why did you hold your tongue?'

I wasn't alone. There were three of us. Three nine-year-old girls who took up jogging to keep ourselves trim because Nadia Comaneci was a tiny little girl and our gymnastics coach warned us that we were in danger of getting fat. And so we jogged past Ben Billman's house until the day he invited us in to see his new caravan and we all went in and we all sat obediently while he stretched our leotards aside and peered at us and pressed his face to our private part, the soft little crease.

One at a time we sat obediently on the strange little bed he had in there; one at a time we sat at the bench and didn't look at each other's faces; and one at a time, when we left his caravan, we agreed we would never speak of it again.

It wasn't me but Lisa O'Daniel who told. It was her mother who called the police. They knocked on the door of the house we rented from Ben Billman, a lady and a man police officer, and they sat outside with me and my mother and two of the sisters, and asked me all the questions, and later my mother said that Lisa O'Daniel had always been a liar and was I sure I wasn't making this up to go along with her.

After that, my mother went to bed, her head beneath the covers as she wept and wept for days.

When I swing the machete in my imagination, his head topples, and then I swing it through his whole house: his wife is sliced in two, his pilot certificates are shredded, his leather recliner chairs are sliced into belt-sized pieces and with the strips of leather recliner I tie them up, both of them, all of them, the remains of them, and then I burn the house down and I stand outside and scream and scream and scream.

But I don't have a machete, I don't have a sword, I don't have a knife. I just have words. Thousands and thousands of them, and each time I swing another one, now, decades after all this, I feel my stomach tighten and the fear rise. It wasn't the first time I wished I'd held my tongue, and not the last time I wished I'd kept my eyes closed. There's purpose in letting things lie, reason in letting the silt settle.

AFTER THREE WEEKS on the *Ocean Thief* my palms were crisscrossed with cuts and calluses, I could haul the nets up myself and I had stopped counting out time in hours. We woke, gathered on deck and called across the escalation of the engines as the nets dropped in; we watched the sun come up and we watched it set. There were snatches of sleep, and then pounding at doors, and then we gathered again, hauling up, untying, watching the mass of life, of colour, of skin, toppling into the tray. Music blasted across the deck while we rinsed and scrubbed and sorted. We stumbled from sleep to waking, and our path grew more and more erratic as the catch got thinner and thinner. On quiet afternoons we folded boxes ready to fill with curved prawns. We folded and folded until Karl told us to stop, because the catch was slow, slower than he'd ever seen it, and we'd be waiting a long time to fill these bloody boxes. Nameless birds flocked on the trawling boom, on the gunwale, on the roof of the wheelhouse. Like the catch, I saw them at first as an unidentifiable mass: wings, beaks, squawking. Black or white, an occasional flash of brown.

At night, when Mick was worn ragged, we took turns on watch, sitting up in the wheelhouse, observing the navigation lights of other trawlers dotting across the water. Alone in the wheelhouse, I felt myself to be finally, perfectly solitary. On deck, I was once more surrounded by moving, jostling male bodies, but here, there was silence and darkness. Just the flashing of the sonar, its vivid green lights a friendly beacon, the soft ping of the radar a comfort. And there was this, too, this perfect gift: the mistakes I made when talking, the awkwardness of being me, saying the wrong words, making the wrong sounds – no one cared on the *Ocean Thief*. Only one thing mattered: were you awake and ready for the catch? Nothing else counted, and it was like being untied. Beyond the wide booms of the *Ocean Thief*, there was perfect liminal space, without boundaries, without restriction. There was the dark curve of the horizon, the kiss of it against the sky. But within that endless space I was contained by fifty feet of steel.

Mick had decorated the wheelhouse with shells and amulets: an amethyst on a cheap gold chain dropped from the ceiling; a faux-antique miniature chest was wedged into the shelf above the desk. Maps of the gulf, shaded in blues and browns, covered the table, and I traced my fingers over the lines that delineated the borders of property, of ownership, of territory. At the side of the table, a pine shelf was attached to the wall, each shelf fitted with its own railing so that the books and objects wouldn't fall. There were no novels, just books on boats, game fishing, one on zoology. A paperback of *How to Win Friends and Influence People*, so battered that the cover had torn completely off. On my second night on watch – in my third week on board – I found a dusty hardback on the bottom shelf, half hidden by a child's kaleidoscope. *The Handbook of Australian Seabirds*. The pages were sweet with the smell of high-quality glossy paper. With the fine beam of pale light overhead, I pored over the photographs until my shift was over and Davey clambered up the ladder, a cup of instant soup in his hand, and then I took the book with me, slipping it into the gap beside my bunk and the cool hull, my wall.

Streaked shearwater. Lesser frigatebird. Caspian tern. In the quiet hours between catching and trawling, between waking and sleeping, I watched the birds lining up along the metal boom and began to name them. The forked tail of the frigatebird. The black hood of the tern. Cross-legged, my back against the sun-warmed wheelhouse, I pressed my fingers to the page, peering at the likenesses. Given names, given titles, the birds emerged into shapes, became less formless. Sometimes, an eastern osprey hovered above us, keeping perfect pace. One roseate tern returned each day, wherever we were, and stayed rooted to the boom while the wind buffeted it. Its wings spread wide when we were trawling, the long tail feathers trailing like kite strings as it sidled closer to the hull, looking down, waiting for our catch. One afternoon, Karl squatted beside me, asked what I was reading. Wordlessly, I flipped the cover closed and showed him the title. He said, 'You into birds?'

The cover was warm in my hands. 'Not really. I just – there's something powerful about knowing the names of things. About being able to name what is in front of you.'

I thought of me and Sylvie listening to her father's old Bob Dylan album, from the Messianic years, the low wailing voice listing the naming of the animals. Pig. Bear. Bull. Like a child's version of Genesis. We thought it was ridiculous. Ridiculous words, ridiculous old voice. I had not yet learned the importance of naming, had not yet understood what putting words to things might mean, what power it might give me, how it might teach me to see.

Karl looked at me, quiet. Then he said, 'Kacey, Robbie's got a girlfriend. I mean, another girlfriend.'

'I know.' I squinted out at the boom. A Caspian tern joined the flock, the beak a cheerful red pointer. I pointed to it. 'Look – see how it's got a different hood from the others?'

Karl stayed sitting next to me, watching the tern sidling along the metal. I glanced at him, wondering whether it had been his idea to suggest this job to me, to get me out here on the

Ocean Thief, away from land, away from Robbie, or whether it had been Robbie's. It didn't matter. I was here, on board, and I wasn't going back.

There was no book in the wheelhouse shelves that told me what the fish were that we hauled out and threw back in as mere waste, not useful for our purposes: the smooth silvery ones, the ones with sharp pointed spines, the ones with narrow long eyes. There wasn't a book to give me a name for my own particular pain, the set of things that had led me there, onto that boat. But I knew my own names, some of them at least. When I was eight, one of my Christmas books was a satisfying hardback, a gift from my father's new wife, called *Hebe's Daughter*. The girl in the book – who became a teenager, then a woman – was called Elizabeth, and Betty, and Hebe's daughter. Different names for different people.

When I was seven – before I read *Hebe's Daughter*, before my father found his new wife – I waited with other kids in the afternoons to catch a bus. Because we had a new house, away from my father, and I had to catch the bus from my old school to my new house. The bus stop was in front of a pub, the Commercial, with individual balconies above the street. Inside the pub, in a dark room on the first floor, my father stayed, and in the afternoons he came out to his own balcony and waved to me or called me inside. Once, he let me have lemonade from the pub, in a round glass with *Commercial Hotel* engraved on the side and a special paper umbrella.

And in those afternoons, while I waited for the bus in front of the Commercial Hotel, if anyone came near me, if anyone spoke to me or asked me where I lived or called me names that I did not choose, I bit them. My father saw me bite a bigger boy and he lifted me up in front of the other kids and stared down at my face and he called me a little fury and I puffed up with pride. After that, the big kids called me Little Fury, or sometimes Little Cannibal. Each time they said it, I bared my teeth and growled, warning them off.

How satisfying it was, to drive my teeth against their flesh, to feel the resistance of muscle. I remember this: grinding my teeth, as though I were a dog, eating raw meat, biting harder and harder. And the victory, to see a perfect curve of teeth, my brand, my warning. I was little, with blonde pigtails, but I wanted to leave the red imprint of my teeth. This is what I remember: the pleasure of giving vent to my fury, the certainty that my wild, hungry anger would protect me. Pleasure in their shock, that someone so little, so cute, so blonde, could run at them with such rage, could long to draw blood, to eat them whole. *Little Cannibal. Little Fury.* How I gloried in those names, how I felt I'd earned them, how I felt they would save me.

Aunty June's porch is like a square stage opening to the theatre of lawn, distinguished with grass, flowerbeds and a wooden seesaw. Sally and I stand on the seesaw instead of sitting, and sometimes she pushes me off and calls me stupid. But I am not stupid because my ladder of words will get me out of here, out of Boolaroo, way past the sky, way above the moon.

Aunty June says the word first, standing with her hand on my mum's arm, leaning in close and whispering to her. She has given me the last of a peanut butter jar and I am dipping my spoon in, dip, dip. 'It was a shocking pain,' Aunty June says – and here her voice goes soft and dreamy – 'in my vagina.'

I think of a beautiful girl, *my* little girl, who would fly above the whole of Boolaroo. She would have long golden hair and she would wear white maxi dresses with pink frills on the bottom. My spoon goes down to the jar, rests there. The peanut butter is thick and sweet in my mouth, and I have to swallow to form the words.

'Vagina,' I say. 'That's a beautiful name. If I have a daughter one day, I will call her Vagina.'

The pause is terrible. My spoon makes a soft clunk on the lino. Beside me is my little red case, ready for me to take across the road to our house with the lock-up. It has a black handle, slippery and shiny, and inside the case there is only my bear, Yogi.

Aunty June and my mother are staring right at each other, and their shoulders shake in the way that grown-ups do when they want to be stupid. Eyes on each other, hands over mouths, little laughing shaking shoulders.

At home, my mother says to the biggest of the sisters: 'Vagina. She wants to call her daughter Vagina!' And they both laugh some more. Outside the steps are cool, and if I sit at the bottom of the steps, I can't hear them in the kitchen cackling and laughing. Vagina! Vagina! Vagina!

I shuffle down to the bottom step and keep my eyes on the top of the lock-up door. There's a drunk in there tonight; I can't see his face, only his finger, sliding up and down around the bars, and I call out to him, 'Hello!'

'Is that a little girl?' he says right back, and I say, 'Yes, it is me, a little girl.'

His face pops up at the bars then. Mauve in the last light, his face is like the cartoon with the strange words and the mole that keeps getting hit. Long and droopy and with a nose that goes all the way down his face, all the way to his chin, and even though he is a man and a grown-up, he is crying in the lock-up. We sit together, the prisoner and me, listening to the cackling from the kitchen and feeling the sky unfolding over Boolaroo. When the dark comes right down, he sings me a song about Saint Peter and a company store. And then I teach him a song I learned from Lisa on *Adventure Island*, and then we sit in silence, but his face drops down so all I can see is his finger holding tight to the bars. One of the sisters brings him food on an enamel prisoner's plate – baked beans and egg and toast that my mum has cooked for him – and tea in a white enamel mug, and then the sister says I have to go inside.

Inside I can't breathe. I try to think about my daughter Vagina and how kind I will be to her, but when I see her in the white maxi dress now my stomach twists with something sour

169

and I only see Aunty June with her hand on my mum's arm. Now, I will call my daughter Lisa after *Adventure Island*. Or perhaps I will call her Clown. Or Flowerpot.

Cunt is later. The first time, I'm still in infants' school. A teenage boy offers me a ride on his bike. I sit on the bar in front of him. He says, 'Do you know what a cunt is?'

'Yes,' I say. Unwilling to admit that I don't know, that I am after all a little kid, I think of what it sounds like – cup! – and declare, 'It's something you drink from.'

The boy laughs, and although it's a nasally mean laugh, when he says, 'Do you want me to show you?' I say yes, because I don't know what else to say and because I want to know all the words. It's not painful. I'm not sure it's even shocking. With one hand on the handlebar, the boy slides his hand into the leg of my cottontail knickers. One finger slides the length of my crease and into what I can only assume is my *cunt*.

I keep my hands on the handlebar. Red tape is wound about the bar and I worry at the tape with my nails. When the boy drops me at the end of my street, I notice that I have red flecks of tape inside my fingernails. I scrub at them in the bath that night, but they remain, small wormish shreds that stay beneath my nails for days.

It was a rare day. There'd been a catch overnight, a full net dropping into the tray while the stars beamed bright and friendly. Daylight was golden and alive, and we cut through the gulf on a steady sea. My arms were forming into muscle, my calves strong from standing all day, and there was a calm on the boat and sunshine pouring yellow across the *Ocean Thief*.

I'd climbed up to the wheelhouse deck and was lying with my bikini top untied, my head resting on my arms. My shadow stretched down the length of the wheelhouse ladder. Beneath my shoulder, the curve of my breast swelled like a small world. I tried to imagine a painting of it, tried to imagine painting it myself. It seemed extraordinary in that moment, the way the world appeared through the triangle of sight between breast and arm, the roundness of me like a mountain, powerful, crushing. And then, when I looked away from the peeling hull beneath me, just glanced through the armpit and into the sea, and felt the sun stroking me: I could be anywhere. With this view, this sifting glisten of light on water, the ocean sun baking us: I could be on the yacht, I could be a millionaire's daughter, I could be anyone. One of those Vaucluse judge's kids, the one who'd grown up in a mansion on the harbour, or the surgeon's son I house-shared with. They'd met at one of the residential colleges, shared stories formed under the old stones, the banners with names listed on them, including the

171

names of their own parents. I watched and listened, learned what to be ashamed of, what to apologise for, what to order for dinner; I watched so carefully you might think I was one of them.

There was a moment, years after I had left the *Ocean Thief*, at a dinner in Oxford. My host was sandy-haired, with a long, angular body, the ease of the natural sportsman, the charm of the natural host. I'd taken my shoes off, as I often do, and tucked my feet up on the sofa. These were good friends. We spent many evenings together; my toddlers played with their pre-schoolers, gazing adoringly at the big kids. My friend went to a boarding school where he was required to wear a tailcoat, and from there to one of the better Oxbridge colleges. He grew up with people like himself and, to him, I appeared to be in more or less the same camp. By the time I came to be sitting on his sofa, I was a writer with some awards under my belt; I taught writing for the University of Oxford; I knew how to round out my vowels and which fork to use. We were talking, that evening, about British politics, about the politics of class. Casually, I said, 'Well, growing up in a working-class family —' I didn't mean 'working class', of course; I meant 'poor'.

I didn't get to finish the sentence. My friend leaned forwards, his hand resting on his denim-covered knee. Astonished, he said, 'Were your family working class?'

Playfully, I tapped him on the chest, asked him if it was a shock to have a member of the proletariat in his living room. Laughing, I told him that I'd get my shovel and coat and go. I was not – am not – so foolish as to believe that he was spared childhood pain by virtue of inherited wealth, or through generations of education, or as a result of never having to think about where, or how, you might live; never having to think about what you might eat, never being at the mercy of someone else's wealth. No. There was, I know, plenty of pain. But I was startled then, and startled now, by the discomfort of the conversation and by the way his response to me shifted afterwards. He was careful with me after that, but his surprise should not have been so unexpected. Like a snake shedding skin, there was nothing of my old self I wanted, nothing of this time of my life I'd carried with me. Like any good runaway, I'd kept my origin story perfectly hidden.

But here, now, there was just this: my body, the view through the gap between breast and arm. A triangle of sky, and the shard of the A-frame slicing it. I whispered the words to myself: *winch, shot, bow, A-frame*. When I was in year five at Biddabah Public School, we had a school camp. Somehow, that year, there'd been one less house move, one less car crash, one less blowout. And, for the first time, there was enough money for the school camp. We stayed in a muddy camp site, watching rain sheet down for five days, sliding down the muddy banks, flinging mud at each other and shrieking with laughter. I didn't feel alone, or strange. And we all slept together, all the girls in the whole class, in an A-frame cabin. We just called it the A-frame, and I loved it. A-frame. It meant only good things to me, only happiness. I whispered it again.

I mouthed all the words, with the sun baking into my lips: *winch, chain, tray, sonar, galley, cabin*. These ordinary words that defined the world I was now contained by. How strange it was that the world stretched beyond the horizon.

Above the deck, above the galley and the narrow cabin space, the A-frame loomed cathedral-like. It was the scaffold for our livelihood, the hold for the nets. At each shot, we winched up and watched the haul suspended from the frame, squirming bodies, mouths and eyes mashed against the net while I tried to look away, while I tried to think of another story, a better one. And then, the untie, and the drop and the frenzy.

I sat up, tying my bikini – stolen from a small boutique in Woollahra, along with a leather anklet that I gave away – and looked up at them, Karl and Davey, laughing. Now, when I remember this day, I have to reach for it, though I remember the sensation of it so clearly. They come slowly into focus, as though I am watching them through water, or blinding sunlight. Voices first: Karl racketing and shouting up there on the frame, his brown legs loose as clouds. Davey, thick and funny, beside him, dared on. My own face is still in shadow, my own name still an invention. I can't quite see myself, I kept myself so hidden.

The skipper had stopped the engines, and the world stretched out beyond us. The container of the *Ocean Thief* was boiling me, suffocating me. Mick clambered out to the deck, miming an exaggerated clown shuffle, lifting his feet and making oooch aah noises; so desperate to be liked, so eager to please, that I had to look away.

Karl climbed to the top of the frame hand over hand until he was a smear against the vivid sky, an electric line, drawn by a master. He called down, 'Do you dare me?' and I called that I did, of course I dared him, and he was in the air, limbs flying like streamers, before the words were out of my mouth, before the skipper had raised his hands in protest.

'Jesus Christ and Mary! Get back on the boat, you fucktard.' Even under pressure, Mick's obscenities seemed learned, performed rather than felt.

Water shot up into the air, and I held my hands out to get some of its cool sweetness. I could hear Karl calling me to come on in, to jump, just jump, and even skinny Davey stood on the lower tip of the frame, arms spread-eagled before he toppled, fell the forty feet down like a straight pin into the desperate blue, and bobbed up again calling me with a dare, a double dare, to jump in, to join in.

Fury

I was slipping out of my denim cut-offs, kicking the battered sandals from my feet, when the hatch to the engine room lifted open and Frenchie peered up at me. He hated to be outside, with the harshness of this northern sun, the constant light. Even at night, when it was cooler and the night a deep purple, lit only by the stars and the moon, he scuttled away from the decks, preferring to be in the huddle of the galley and the dark noise of the engine room. I assumed he had a stash of whisky down there, because in spite of the fact that the *Ocean Thief* was a dry boat his eyes maintained the tinge of red on the rims, set off by a yellow on the whites, that identified him as a habitual drinker. Light was unpleasant to him; he blinked into it the way I imagined a mole might, scratching its way up from the cool loamy earth. He sniffed the air a little, said, 'Why the swimming suit? This water is not for swimming in. It's dangerous.'

'Why are you on a boat, if you hate water and light so much?' I stood on the long gunwale, the soles of my feet burning.

Frenchie shook his head, as though dislodging water. 'This is a good job. Good pay when the catch is good. Soon I'll retire, anyway.'

He did not say, This is a good place to hide. But now I know that's what he meant.

He stared down at the water, hand over his eyes to shield himself from the light, and said again, 'It's dangerous.'

I said, 'The boys are in there.'

'Exactly.'

It was a joke, of course it was, and so I laughed. Still laughing, I climbed hand over hand up the metal frame, with the chants of 'jump, jump, jump' ricocheting up at me. Rust peeled beneath my nails, and I was suddenly aware of the flimsiness of my bikini, of the way the back of it crept up, exposing my butt cheeks, the way the string barely held the triangles of fabric in place. From the edge of the frame, the water looked terrifyingly far away. But sunlight bounced off it and the crisp cool blue was so smooth, the shine of it inviting. Davey and Karl were still chanting from the water, and down on deck the skipper was still shouting. I grazed my back on the beam as I dropped down, feeling the air rush over me. The fall felt long, and my arms waved in the air as though I were trying to fly. Water smacked hard against me, then gave way. I dropped down, straight and true, and kept dropping until the water turned dark and cold and squeezed on my eyes. *I felt the wet push its black thumb-balls in, the night you died.* Did I think of 'Five Bells' then, or only later? Everything pressed on me and still I seemed to torpedo down, down. Somehow, finally, an inkling, a memory of my body, and I kicked, reached, swam for the circle of light and emerged gasping, victorious, brave like a boy.

I DON'T KNOW WHY they came that day and not another. I suppose they were always there, shooting about under the surface. My lungs were still tingling with the leap into the sea when we dropped the nets in, trawling up and down the long trench of the gulf, dolphin pods flipping and dipping behind us. The laughter and hooting fell away from us once we brought the nets up: another catch full of everything but what we wanted, everything but money. Slime caught between my toes in the manky lining of my boots, the board shorts I'd borrowed from Karl flapped above my knees, and the catch was washed away down the chute. Schools of long thin fish, round silver fish, puffers, baitfish; everything but prawns. Davey put some Cold Chisel on and I didn't have it in me to argue, so Jimmy Barnes hollered about flame trees and the girl he'd left behind, while I watched and waited, my raspberry-red gloves hovering above the tray, ready to grab the spiky stripes of the tiger prawns. Mick had relaxed, or perhaps abandoned hope for a time, and so the *Ocean Thief* was not powering through the water at speed and we waited on deck, legs akimbo, gloved hands hovering, fighting over the grabbing of the odd single prawn. I thought about my ticket out of there, and the money I needed to get it, and I watched the water wash the baitfish down the tray and into the chute, spitting them back into the sea.

In photos of English summers, there were always meadows or woods, blanketed with small flowers: bluebells, daisies, buttercups. Here, that meadow was the wide azure expanse of the Arafura Sea, and the flowers were dead fish, floating on their sides, scales sparkling in the sun. Watching the diamonds of light glinting you'd think they were life; you'd think they were nothing but beauty. Flowers spread out for a princess.

Mick noticed them first. Up there in the wheelhouse, he could see for miles, scanning to the horizon, watching the light shift and change. He'd watched the spread of fish, the blanket of dead sea life, hauled up from the depths, left to dry in the air and then thrown back as waste. This was what we did, what we were. Mick thought nothing about the fish, thought only about the catch, the money that he wasn't bringing in. He thought about the uncle who owned the fleet, the uncle who had promised him a chance, and how spectacularly he was managing to screw it up with his thinning catch, his disobedient engineer, his incompetent deckhands. He didn't think about sharks until he saw them. On the periphery at first, the usual scattering of reef sharks, come for the feast. Then, the saw-tooth sharks, mouths open like cartoons of *Jaws*, their great curved heads making half-moons as they skimmed the fish, barely rippling the water. By the time he hollered to us to get to the bow, to come and look, there were scores of them: hammerheads, grey nurses, white pointers, tiger sharks. Oblivious to us and to each other, they skimmed back and forth, forming a spectacular community, a city of sharks. Reef sharks dipped under and up, snatching the small bait trails. Blacktips flipped beneath the bellies of indifferent bull sharks and threshers, their dorsal fins making smooth zigzags through the water. I tried to count but they kept moving and there were so many of them. I stopped counting at forty-two. Mick took the cigarette out of his mouth, a flicker of ash making a dandruff-sized spot on his beard until the wind picked it up. 'See why I wasn't keen on your jumping game today?' He stubbed the cigarette out, flicked the butt to the sharks. 'They're always there.'

I kept my eyes on the water. 'Everything has to eat, Mick.'

He nodded. 'But I don't want to be their food. And I don't want to have to go into Darwin minus a crew member.'

Behind him, Karl's voice cut across the dusk. 'They're beautiful.'

'Beautiful bastards. Murderous.'

'No, mate. They're always in there, but how many times have you been bitten? How many times have I? And I spend half my life in the water.'

Mick wasn't giving in, though. 'Knew a bloke in Geraldton, got his leg taken. Fricken white pointer.'

Karl's eyes were dots of shine in the lowering light. 'Mate, you can't blame a whole species for that.'

Some, only some. Mick slipped back into the wheelhouse, started up, and the bow dipped a little as the engine took hold. I watched the water ruffle and rise ahead of me. Four men on a boat and me, and not one of them intending to do me harm. Not because I was sober, and not because I was not wearing silky underwear. Not because of anything I did or did not do. I simply was not their prey.

I stayed on the bow deck until the light left, watching them take it all, until the surface was only scattered with innards and thin trails of blood, and then we hauled up and started again, up and down all through the night.

ON THOSE WILD nights when the wind whipped the waves into a frenzy, we felt only freedom. Airborne, wind making a choral harmony outside, my arms up, my legs loose. Flying, that was what it felt like. Beneath me, the floor of the galley rose up again, and I arrived, softening my knees the way I'd learned to in primary school gymnastics lessons. Another swell, the tub of the *Ocean Thief* riding up the wave, teetering on the smooth crest and dropping down. In that instant, the second between arrival at the crest and dropping to the base of the next swell, we jumped. Me, Karl and Davey, shrieking like kids. This might be the closest I would get to flight, the nearest I could get to freedom. At first, when the wind hammered and howled and the boat started to teeter on the wild swell, fear swelled in me, equal to the storm. Large enough to swallow me up. But, as it grew, Karl demonstrated the leaping-flying technique: jumping into the air as the boat rose, and the drop down giving a moment of flying.

Too wild to sleep, and too dangerous to winch the nets up; we squeezed around the galley table while Frenchie made hot chocolate that splashed across our faces. We shared more stories, and I swallowed them up, took them into my own self, and then the wind slowed, and we went out on deck. Moonlight made white patches against the A-frame and my chorus of terns teetered on the booms, their feet curved around the narrow bars.

It was the moonlight, not our own artificial beams, that showed up the sword sticking through the net as we began to haul it up. That deep teardrop of net, fat and full of fish layered on top of each other, eyes pressing, bodies twitching. Halfway down, a swordfish: as large as a shark, its long, serrated sword breaking the line of the catch. I swear I could see its eye looking up at me.

Karl hung over the gunwale, peering down at the net. With each lift, each turn of the winch, the catch plunged a little more. When a woman is about to give birth, the baby descends into the cervix, easing its way down into the pelvic area, engaged, ready to travel through the birth canal. And this is what the net was like, the catch engaging, weight dragging. With each shift, each drop, the swordfish serrated the net, tearing bigger and bigger holes, risking the whole catch. Over the thump of the engine, Karl was shouting something, calling for Frenchie to bring his machete.

'Kacey, go down to the engine room and get Frenchie. I need his machete.'

I hollered back. 'Why?'

He was still draped over the gunwale and turned his head back so that his hair twirled out like a skirt. He hid nothing, ever, Karl. I could see the snap in him. 'For real? Just get it.'

I backed away, but I hated that engine room with its dark and heat and constant engine churn. I hated being closed in. I hated the feeling that I couldn't escape, that I was trapped, that the noise would press in on me, escalating the noise in my own head.

Davey put his hand on my wrist. 'I'll go.' He clambered down the ladder to the engine room while the boat rocked.

We didn't hear him fall, didn't hear the thud or call or crack of bone. We only felt the lurch of the *Ocean Thief* when another wave hit; my feet slid from under me and I grabbed at the tray, pulled myself to standing. Another rise, another fall, and it was

Frenchie who climbed out of the engine room and handed Karl the knife.

Karl said, 'Where's Davey?'

Frenchie nodded back at the engine room hatch, said, 'He went on his arm. It cracked. The boy is crying. Here is the knife.'

And behind him, Davey, holding his arm across his waist. He was pale in the pearly light on deck, doubled over and moaning.

'What happened?'

'Fell on my arm. It's – I think it's broken. I can't – it really hurts. I'm sorry.'

'What for?'

'If we have to go in . . .'

'We won't. I'm sure we won't. I guess we – I mean, a splint? We could bandage it?'

'Help Karl first.'

But Karl was already crabbing along the trawling boom. The water had calmed a little, and he'd strapped the knife to his belt. Glinting in the moonlight, it looked ready to slice his leg. The sword of the fish was halfway down the net, sandwiched between tonnes of fish still – for the moment – living, flipping, flailing. Below the boom, the boards dangled, a loose platform. When the nets went in, these boards parted, holding the mouth of the net open. When the nets were lifted, the boards hung below the boom, moving but stable. Karl lifted himself down to the board, while Frenchie and I watched anxiously from the safety of the deck and Davey doubled over, holding his wounded arm.

Karl scrambled down, his arms hanging below the boards, reaching down to the net. Still not close enough, he stretched his body out and swung from the net itself, slicing, sawing at the sword of the living creature caught there until, with a savage cut, he tore it free. In the dark, I couldn't see the blood, but I knew it was there, and when Karl climbed back onto the deck, holding the sword aloft like a prize, I couldn't look at him.

'What?' he said. 'What did you think I was going to do?'

'I thought you were going to release it. Let it go.'

'How? Why?'

'I don't know how.' I was shouting now, my throat tight. 'But you'd do it because you're a decent person. Because we're here to catch prawns, not – I mean, it's like a dolphin – it's—' And there I was, crying, like a baby, like a girl.

'Don't be such an idiot, Kacey. What did you think we were here for? How did you think you were going to get what you wanted without killing some fish, for fuck's sake?' It was the first time, the only time, that I saw Karl's face change with anger. 'How about thank you? I didn't notice you going out to solve the problem.'

'I'd have opened the nets.'

'Then you're definitely an idiot.'

'And you're a brutal fucking bastard.'

'You're crying for one fish. It doesn't even make sense.'

It was true. It didn't. And I didn't have the words, not properly, to say that it was easier to feel compassion for one creature suffering in front of you then it was to feel compassion for a whole species, for several species. I hadn't properly understood that compassion was not weakness. Words were simple tools for Karl, designed to do one simple job; he didn't have the word *hypocrite* in his vocabulary, but I did. I shouted again, 'You're a brutal bastard,' and I'd have stormed off like a teenager, slamming the door behind me, but there was nowhere to storm to. We still had a full net to haul in and to sort, a full night's work ahead. I tried to keep my anger fuelled, topping it up with a list of injustices, but Karl had let it go before the catch was fully in, letting it swim away from him with no trace.

PLASTIC AND SHINY, the red needle slicked slightly in my sweaty hand. Legs stuck out in front of me, the weight of the net crushing on my knees, I watched Karl, mimicking the way his hand slipped under and over, knotting quickly. He squatted, his fingers moving like fish through the net. Davey had turned a tub upside down and sat on it primly, the net falling away from him like a wedding dress train, his bandaged arm with the improvised splint folded uselessly on his lap.

It wasn't holes in the nets causing a lack of catch, Karl said, it was dodgy finding, bad storms and too many, way too many, boats in the gulf. But the swordfish – he turned his body away from me, looked down at the needle in his hand – the swordfish had made a fierce bloody hole. In spite of everything.

At night, during so many nights, we watched the lights of scores of trawlers dropping in and out, signalling to each other. During those nights, and the days that led to them, I huddled in my bunk, or on the upper deck, watching my terns on the booms, the ones I had come to know, and I scribbled in my journals. I'd brought three of them with me, hard-backed, with cream-coloured pages, lined in grey. Contained by the *Ocean Thief*, crowded in by the sea and by storm, memories were swirling up at me. I had nowhere to put them but on the page, trying to wrestle them back to silence, back to invisibility, where I'd kept them for so many years.

Fury

Sometimes, we heard news of one crew or another. Bad news usually, flickering across the water like light. One of the old trawlers from a Cairns fleet had flipped and only three of the crew were found alive. Three boats from a rival fleet had gone into shore, abandoning the dubious catch after the last clutch of storms. A police boat had gone out to the *Sea Beast* and three marine cops climbed on board. Word had travelled via the radio that something was up, and Frenchie squinted at the action through his binoculars while Mick told him to mind his fucking business. The cops were on board, their white and blue boat tied alongside the *Sea Beast*, its booms dipping up then down. After minutes – half an hour perhaps, maybe longer – the police climbed back down onto their boat, taking with them the cook, wrapped in a reflective blanket. On that day, I'd slapped Frenchie on the leg, said, 'How do you know it's the cook?' He kicked me away as though I were a fly and said, 'It's a girl.'

'You're not a girl, Frenchie, and you do the cooking on our boat.'

'That's only because you are a very bad cook.'

I'd grinned up at him. 'But a very good deckhand.'

Frenchie looked down at Karl then, eyebrows raised, and Karl shrugged. 'Not a completely useless deckhand.' He paused. 'Not the worst deckhand.'

When the police boat sped away, making a wide white wake, taking the blanket-wrapped cook with them, I'd climbed up to my perch on the upper deck. Huddled near the boom, I watched the terns and frigatebirds buffeted by the wind, and I thought about the girl with the marine policeman's arm about her, and although I did not know, not really, what had happened to her, I felt unreasonably grateful for the simple fact of being on a boat with four men who would not hurt me. I was swollen with gratitude because they chose to honour the most basic of human exchanges.

Now, with the net spread across our knees, Karl said, 'We were all blokes on my first boat. No girls.'

I wondered what his point was. No girls to shout and cry and carry on and *make a fuss*? There was just me and Karl and Davey on the deck; Mick was holed up in his cabin or the wheelhouse, too unsure of his own authority to hang with us. And Frenchie: who knew where he was at any time? In the galley with a dirty checked tea towel tied about his waist or hiding out in the engine room. I'd been down there twice, only twice. Cloistered in that dark and hot space, where the engine thrummed and sweltered, I thought I would suffocate. For Frenchie, it was as inviting as a womb.

Davey tucked his bandaged wrist into his belly. For the fifth time, or the sixth, he said, 'I'm sorry I can't help. Stupid—' He looked down at the improvised splint. 'So fucking clumsy.'

'It's okay, Davey.' To Karl, I said, 'No girls, huh? How did that end up? Good catch?'

His curls shook.

'We sank.'

I tied off the net, my knot a messy lump in the centre. 'Sank metaphorically? Or sank for real?'

'What the fuck's *metaphorically* mean?' Karl's teeth were neat little squares; his mouth made the shape of an arrow when he smiled. 'We sank. The nets were lodged, the boat went over, took water and went under. We sat in the tender, waiting, until another trawler came along and then we hitched a ride with that. They were all pissed, and we drank what was left of their bourbon, then passed out in the wheelhouse.'

'Jesus. I mean – what happened?'

'I just told you. We sank.'

'That's it? You really know how to spin a story.'

He laughed. 'I come from a storytelling people.'

Davey snorted. 'It must have skipped you, mate.'

Stripes of shade and sun danced across the deck and across our legs, lazy heat baking into our bones. I slung the net across my lap. 'Yeah. Skipped a generation, or the gene mutated.'

Davey tilted his head at me. I could almost see his ears cocking. He'd left school at fifteen, and missed the knowledge that I took for granted, that I'd hungered for, that I held close to me, hoarding it. Trying to make my eyes glint mysteriously, I said, 'I come from a storytelling people too.'

'What? White trash?' Karl was, I suppose, allowed to say it because I'd said it once to him, jokingly. But still it stung.

'Great-grandfather William was a German Jew.' But the truth was, I knew nothing of him, not of any of them, and I didn't want to have to answer to them. I returned to the sinking. 'Was the boat salvaged?'

'Nah. Under without a trace. With my best fucking sneakers.'

'But you wanted to come back for the next season?'

'Fuck, yeah. What else would I do?'

I thought back to the night around the galley table, with that question burning: why, why are you here? And the only answer, for all of us: there's nowhere else I can go. I tugged the last knot on the net and slung it back to the deck, wriggled my legs. Like doo-wop backing singers, Davey and I repeated Karl's refrain. 'Fuck, yeah.'

We laughed as we said it, in unison like that, and held up our hands like schoolkids, linking fingers, calling 'Jinx, jinx, double-jinx,' and we were still laughing when Mick clambered down the ladder to the stern deck. We stopped laughing quickly; he had that effect. It wasn't that we were frightened of him, but that we felt sorry for him, for the way he stood on the fringe all the time, his hands tapping at his belt, his beard twitching while he decided whether to speak or remain mute. He nodded at Karl and said, 'Right. We're going to head down to Bonaparte.'

At the tip of Australia there are two long promontories. As a child, they seemed elegant to me, a perfect balance, appearing on maps as twin daggers. Between these two capes is the Gulf of Carpentaria. On the western side of one of these points – the Northern Territory – is Bonaparte Gulf, leading into the Timor Sea. Named for Joseph, Napoleon's brother. There are two seasons for trawling: one, during the winter storms, is in the exposed Bonaparte Gulf. Here are the fat banana prawns. By the end of winter, the boats move to Carpentaria, and to the thinner tiger prawns. We were now in the season for tigers.

The last of Karl's laugh dropped away, sank. He dropped the net to the deck but stayed squatting, his bare feet solid on the deck. 'Bonaparte? Why?'

'We're not catching anything here.' Mick nodded towards the boats surrounding us. 'Too much competition. No one's down in Bonaparte.'

'That's because the season there is over. Bananas ended two months ago.'

'Six weeks ago. We can catch the back end of it.'

'We're here to catch tiger prawns. It's tiger season. We're not taking banana prawns back. Anyway, we'll be too exposed in the storms.' Karl stood up, folded his arms. 'Seriously, skipper, there's a reason no boats are down in Bonaparte.'

Mick shook his head. 'Yep, well, as you say, I'm the skipper, and we're going to Bonaparte.'

'We'll lose four days' fishing to get there.'

'It's worth it. Can't be worse, anyway.'

But, as was the case with so many things, he was wrong.

HE TAKES THE STAND. His cheeks are round. Dark hair covers his chin. Thick shoulders, thick hands. Meaty: that's the word you would use to describe his hands, the word I would use. Someone has advised him well on his wardrobe; I look over to his wife, small, dark-haired, her legs neatly crossed at the ankles. He wears a navy tie that matches almost perfectly the dress she wears. He says, 'I thought to myself, well, she is a pretty girl, but that is all. I would not even kiss her unless she said yes.' He shrugs, smiling, and the jury look over at me. Sitting opposite his wife, I'm aware that I will seem plump, my arms flabby despite the weeks of barely eating. Despite those dieting days, my chin has an extra layer, an almost-double that wobbles when I turn my head too quickly. I watch the shine on his face as he speaks, his mouth wet and troubling beneath the thick beard. On the other side of the courtroom, his wife dabs at her eyes. Her nails are long, painted shell-pink.

I am not on trial, the prosecutor said. But already the jury are comparing us. His delicate fine-boned wife, newly emigrated to be with her husband, and me, with anger blazing in every scrape of my hair, every red blotch on my face. It's true, when I tied my hair back, resisting any instinct to fluff a tiny fringe out, to *soften* it, I mouthed, 'Fuck you,' at the mirror. If I could stand in the middle of the courtroom and scream those words now, the way I shouted them in the middle of the field while

Tony de Ropp and his idiot friend skidded around me, I would. It worked with those early high school boys, astonished by my breasts, but my anger can't save me now.

My dress is a shiny polyester, an unappealing beige. My chest is bare of jewellery but, anyway, I am covered by the beige polyester, the square neckline cutting at the base of my neck so that not even a trace of chest or clavicle can be seen. I hesitated over black tights – were they too saucy? Too sexy? After all, on the night I got into that taxi my legs were bare below my short skirt, but my boots – it could, and would, be argued – created a deliberately tempting eyeline, a teasing gap between thigh and knee that invited the eye and therefore, inevitably, the hand. If I'd gone looking for the least flattering item of clothing, this would be it. Sexless, schoolmarmish. I bought it the previous year for a fancy-dress party. I went as a public servant. I thought I was hilarious.

Look pretty, a friend said, but not too pretty. I didn't want to look pretty at all, I wanted to scrub myself away. I scraped my hair back into a tight bun. Sleepless for days, my face was puffy, my skin spotty. I wore no make-up. Not too pretty, or not pretty enough.

The friend who told me to look pretty (but not too pretty) was raped when a kid – that was what they called him, although he was twenty-two – broke into her house one morning, looking for cash, but he found her instead.

Last year I read *Lucky*, Alice Sebold's memoir. When she describes her brutal rape, she adds that she was a virgin. And later, the cops report that she was a good girl. This week, I read another report of a recent sexual assault. This was a girl, the report trumpeted, who was innocent, who did not bring this on in any way, who had no cause to expect such a thing. A good girl. In contrast, on the same day there was a story about a thirteen-year-old girl, not a good girl. A runaway, with a twenty-year-old man who, the paper reported, 'had a sexual relationship' with her. You cannot rape a girl who is not a good girl, it seems. Even if she is a child.

I was not a good girl. So perhaps this, all this – the courtroom, the barrister glaring at me, the waiting faces – is what I have a right to expect. If a girl lies and steals and sleeps with people she does not love, what can she expect from the world? What should she expect?

My mother does not come with me to the first day or the second of the trial. I don't want her to. This has always been a marker of my life. In primary school, friends have mothers and fathers sitting in the audience at Easter hat parades, or assemblies. My mother, working shift work, strained and stressed, is never at these events. Once, a sister comes to an Easter hat parade; the other kids cluster around her, asking me if she is my mother.

My mother works late at night and early in the morning, driving forty minutes each way around the lake, dressed in her nurse's aide uniform. When she comes home, she is sad and lonely and tired and broke. When she is not lying awake at night worrying about how to pay the bills, or who will save her, she is working. When she is not working, she is exhausted. And when she is any of these things, she goes to bed, burrowing beneath the covers, whispering that she cannot cope, so could we please just leave her alone for a little while?

In year six, when I receive the little printed card – gold-embossed – that announces me dux of the year, I hold it tightly in my hand, gazing at it alone. With no audience for my achievement, I hoard a secret pleasure, guard a private pride.

And now, I do not know how to ask for support, how to ask for someone to sit with me, to hold my hand and to let me be a child. Although I am not a good girl, I long for comfort. There is no one to tell me that it doesn't look good for me to have no one there to support me. What am I, a waif? Or a girl so wicked that she has no family left to care for her? I think only about what I need to do to shut myself down.

And also, I am ashamed.

When I stumbled into the police station and the horse-faced sergeant told me, wagging his finger, how drunk I was, I knew that he was right. I knew that his subtext – that I should not be believed because I had lost count of how much I'd had to drink – was right. I am, now, in this courtroom, ashamed to be the girl that I am, ashamed to be confronted with my own confusion. After that first time, I sit outside the courtroom when he speaks. I can't bear to listen to him, can't bear to hear them discussing me – my drunkenness, my underpants, my vagina. Later, much later, I understand that this too will work against me.

I sit outside the court on a long wooden bench. Cool to the touch, the wood is smooth, the tiled floor echoing footsteps, amplifying sound. After a few minutes, a wigged barrister scuttles out of a courtroom at the end of a corridor, robe billowing. Papers are cradled to his chest and, as I lift my head to nod at him, the papers slip from his grasp. Black cloth, the trim of his robe, makes a dark cloud behind him as he kneels, muttering under his breath, gathering the papers back to his embrace. When he stands, he shakes his head at me, as though I am the cause of his clumsiness. Blame, in life and in law, can seem unreasonably hard to apportion.

I step back into the courtroom when they call the other taxi driver – Sid – to the stand. 'She was on the road,' he said, 'shouting, blood on her legs, her clothes half trailing behind her.' I sit in the gallery while he is speaking, watching the considered way he moves his hands on the lip of the witness box.

The crown prosecutor asks, 'Can you see the young woman you picked up?'

'Yes.' And he points to me, shaking in the gallery.

Later, the defending prosecutor says, 'When you picked this – girl – up, you say she was distressed, yes?'

'Yes,' the man says. 'I don't *say* it. She was distressed. That's fact.'

The barrister is silky-smooth. Dark hair peeps out from under his wig. His eyebrows are tidy, as though waxed or trimmed; his teeth are white and straight. Long fingers – a pianist's fingers – flick at the bow on his gown. Slowly, he turns, walks towards the dock. 'How did you perceive this distress?'

Sid blows air out, a thin whistle. 'When someone is distressed, it's bloody obvious, isn't it?'

The barrister raises his trimmed, brushed eyebrows. The judge leans towards the dock, says, 'Language.' As though Sid is a toddler or a primary school child presenting his end-of-term speech.

'Perhaps so.' The barrister smiles without showing his teeth. 'But indulge me.'

'She was crying. Her make-up was smeared. She was half in and half out of her clothes. She had blood on her legs. She was standing in the middle of the road waving her arms. Is that bloody distressed enough for you?'

This man. I want to find him, now. I want to thank him.

The barrister smiles again. 'Would it be reasonable to suggest that the complainant was very drunk?'

'I don't—'

'And that many of the signs you suggest – dishevelment, disorientation, personal abandon – that these are also signs of a significant level of intoxication?'

I leave the courtroom, the door thudding behind me. Outside, in the cool corridor, I count the tiles, and then I walk up and down the length of them, listening to the echo of my own footsteps.

What the taxi driver who picked me up says is this. He stopped on the road, leaving his headlights on. Lit up, I was a waving lantern, arms above my head. Unsure of what I was, he approached slowly, getting out of his taxi, holding his hands out in front of him. Palms up, as though I were a wild animal, cornered and dangerous in its fear.

THIS IS WHAT I remember of my first kiss.

The boy's name is Steven, that's what he tells me. The dark has started to drift over the gully behind our new house, and I am roaming like a free girl through the grass. Steven is there from nowhere, walking beside me. Where does he come from? His pretty face is flushed in the cool air, his hair wispy brown, so fine it makes me want to touch it. On the first day of knowing him, he whispers to me, 'Do you want to see a rude word?' I do, I do want to see a rude word, so badly that the thrill of it threatens to swim up through my toes and drown me. It's very quiet and he takes my hand.

The streets of Speers Point are busier than the streets of Boolaroo, although they are emptier, not having my dad in them. His absence fills the whole of the house, the whole of the town. But this is a town just for a little while, not to stay. Until we find another place, until we find our feet.

Outside on the street, there is a telegraph pole, dark at the bottom and pale at the top, so that it looks like it is still a tree, still what it always was, only with someone sticking wires at the top. We whisper as we get closer to the terrible word. We stop respectfully a few feet from the pole and Steven silently and solemnly points to the word, painted there on the pole for everyone to see. I know words, I can read them, and I can read this word: *Dick*. I run my hand down the pole. The word *Dick* is right beneath my skin and my face burns with its charge.

'When did you first notice it?' I ask. I have heard people on television say 'When did you notice this?' instead of 'When did you see it?' and I like the sound of it.

'It's always been here.'

I say, 'The person who wrote it will get in enormous trouble.'

Enormous is a word I am trying out.

Steven steps away from the pole. 'Do you think so?'

I say, 'Well, no one will ever discover who put it there. Anyway, it's always been there, probably.'

Discover is another word I have noticed. On *Adventure Island* Miser Meanie worked hard to discover who took his sweets. (I can tell you: it was him! He hid them himself and then forgot!)

Steven repeats after me: 'No one will discover it.'

'No,' I say. 'They never will.'

And then he says, 'Do you want to kiss?'

'Yes,' I say, because I do want to kiss. I think that we will stand right there, in the middle of the empty field between our new house and the Italians, but we don't. Steven does not hold my hand, but we walk next to each other, carefully not touching, carefully not looking at each other, and we place our feet carefully on the ground. There are no more words to speak so we are quiet, listening to the distance of the cars.

Near the mandarin tree, there's a soft clearing in the grass. Steven lies down there and looks up at me with his wispy brown hair and his speckled brown eyes and he says, 'We have to lie down.'

'To kiss?'

'Yes, that's what they do.'

What who does? But I am already lying beside him, my lips puckering, my arm about his head. His lips are soft, and a little bit of dribble falls from his mouth into mine. I like the feeling of his soft lips and the leafy smell of his breath. I like the weight of him, his skinny arms digging into my ribs. After the kiss we walk back to the road, watching our feet on the grass.

Later that year, the boy next door invites me over. After I have said that no I would not like to F-U-C-K, he puts his soft thing inside my pants anyway, while I stand obediently, staring at the window, and the kookaburra perches on the wire, laughing.

We SHOULD HAVE pulled the nets up when the storm started.

Bonaparte was as empty as Carpentaria. Worse. Along the exposed coast, the winds had buffeted our little boat, slamming waves against the hull. We pitched one way then the other, angling so sharply that the booms on either side were in the water. We motored through the night in a rocky sea, taking turns to sleep and turns to hold the watch with the skipper. During my sleep shifts, I held my hand against the bunk, trying to imagine that the rise and fall was comforting, was a rocking chair, a womb. This was the gift of all those books, all those years of making things up: I could imagine, I could pretend my way out of fear.

Wind still roared about us on the first day, and the second, after we got to the gulf, and our nets twice came up as good as empty. And on the third day the wind strengthened its roar, the water turned a deeper dark. No glorious sunset shifted across the sky, just a grey palette, a rattling of thunder. Karl looked up at the sky, sniffing the air, and called up to Mick in the wheelhouse, 'We shouldn't shoot. It's going to turn bad.' He corrected himself. 'Worse.'

Mick clambered out, standing with legs wide on the tray, hands on his hips, eyes narrowed while he followed Karl's gaze. Karl waited, and then added, 'It looks like it'll be rough, skipper. What do you reckon?'

Mick shook his head and said, 'We can't afford to miss a catch, we're already down. At this rate, we'll go back owing money and I've promised my missus we can buy a house.'

Karl looked out to the darkening horizon, the thick clouds clumping. Thunder boomed somewhere, a distance away. 'You sure?'

Mick nodded. 'I'm absolutely certain. Shoot away.'

Sliding across the deck, rain slapping into our faces, we hauled the nets up and heaved at the ropes, swung them out and down, watching them churn in the waves. The boards held for a moment then stretched apart until the weight of water – and of the boards – dragged the nets down. We huddled in the galley, too nervous to sleep, while thunder escalated around us and Karl told stories of stupid skippers he had known, or known of, before now; the grisly ends they had come to.

First, we heard the rain battering down, then the thunder coming closer, and then the shrieking. High, constant, like a rolling wave; like a human scream, a series of human screams. We ran out on deck, sliding and shouting, unsure of what we'd find, what we could do. There were scores of them, bills snapping up and beneath, silver gleams of backs caught in the snatches of light from the boat. Dolphins trailing the nets, screeching. More and more of them came, the beaks open, the shrieking unbearable. We peered into the dark pulp of the nets while Mick shouted at us to winch up, get the fucking nets up, sure that we'd caught a dolphin in there. Even in those wild days in the gulf, when the laws were lax and loosely policed – even then, to catch a dolphin, to drown it in a net, would not be forgiven.

We tried to pull up, but at each point the nets, heaving and thrashing in the white-capped sea, sagged and dropped. I turned the winch while Karl peered out at the boards, thrashing uselessly, holding the nets down. He shouted across the wind, 'The boards are broken. Drop the winch.'

I couldn't hear him properly, so I kept turning. He ran at me then, skidding a little on the wet deck, shouting louder. 'Stop fucking winching! If we pull up in this, while the boards are broken, it will fricken tip us.'

'What do we do?' I kept my hand on the winch to keep myself steady.

'Fix them. We have to fix them.'

I looked at the white water, at the rolling booms, and I looked back at Karl. He had already stepped out of his gumboots. He nodded at my own boots, shouted, 'You'll have to come out on the boom with me. I need the light.'

I followed him out on the boom, gripping the narrow rail, trying not to look down.

My bare feet curved, my toes gripping the narrow width of the boom holding me unsteadily as the boat lurched. Following Karl's instructions, I'd hooked my arms over the narrow band that formed a sort of rail above the boom. Mouth dry, terror at the back of my throat, I leaned forward, clutching a Dolphin torch in one hand, the beam rising and falling as the wooden boards below me slapped up and down with the slide of the ocean. Waves smacked against the boards with the force of a punch. The metal cut into the softness of my armpits. Framed by the black of the water snapping at his feet, Karl's face flashed in and out of the light. His eyes wide, white; I couldn't let myself notice if what I saw there was fear. If I saw fear in him, I would be lost.

And so, instead of squinting through the spray to the dark and wild shadow of Karl's face, I peered down at my hands, at the messy beam of the torch. The belt of tools at my waist dug into me, the handle of a metal tool – a spanner? a wrench? – stabbing into the flesh at my hip, a relief from the pressure of the boom across my belly. Karl shouted up at me, but his words were whipped away. *Ack. Asser. Ick. Uck.*

It was all noise, a wash and a roar of sound: Karl's snippets, half-words that disappeared into the storm; the punch-roar of the waves; Davey on deck calling *sorrysorrysorry*; the skipper behind him fist-shaking, shouting; my own bloody heart, the thudding of it.

Karl raised his face again as another wave rose. '*The screw.*' A wave interrupted. '*Iver. Need. Mash.*'

Folding myself in two, I leaned further down, a screwdriver dangling from my hand. Karl reached up, but not close enough. Each wave jerked at the heavy nets, lurching the boat this way and that. My foot lifted off the boom, while my arms gripped tighter. On the deck behind me, Davey shouted a warning. The boom lifted then fell and the boards smashed towards me. The torch dropped from my hand just as another wall of water surged, pounding into my face, my eyes, until I was blinded, only feeling the turn of metal beneath me. I grabbed at something near, while the wall of the world – dark, impenetrable – came closer. Terns screeched, counterpointing the shrieking of the dolphins below and the rattling inside my skull, a bass reverberation. Karl's voice sounded below me, a call, a warning, and then there was the clang of the chains and a sudden smack to my face. The thickness of blood then, and an unexpected, momentary blindness.

It was soundless for a moment – a second? A slice of a second? – and so I must have passed out. When I blinked back to consciousness, I was doubled forward, my arms linked over the rail which had held me upright and prevented me tumbling from the boom into the water. Blood, sticky and sweet, was thick on my face, in my mouth. Across the water a sheet of lightning flashed the sky on, then off, and both Davey and Mick were shouting at us to get in, get off the fucking metal boom, there's lightning, just leave it, get the fuck in. Another flash, and Karl hauled himself up next to me, shouting at me to move, to get in, to hurry the fuck up. Rain slapped into my eyes, making my hands slip. When we made it to the deck, there was another lurch and we fell inside the galley: blood on my face, my hands, my teeth.

I trembled all through the night, with the nets in the water ready to drag us under, and the cracking of thunder like a series of punches outside. All night, the storm raged while our nets dragged, each wave and crash escalating the risk of capsize. All night, we took turns with the skipper in the wheelhouse, holding tight, hoping for the best, waiting for the calm to come.

SOLID GROUND was too unyielding. My legs buckled and folded on the carpet, unable to connect properly to the solid floor of the Darwin hotel lobby. I had become used to a constantly moving surface. Now, the earth felt wrong: too settled, too solid, too stable. How quickly we become accustomed to our own circumstances; how easily, how terribly, we adapt. Frogs boiling, lobsters turning pink. As a child, I was accustomed to turmoil and uncertainty. It will be years before I adapt to happiness, to love; years before I stop craving noise, chaos, misery.

The woman at the reception looked at me briefly, her eyes following the trail from eyes to my cheek. Dulled by painkillers, my cheeks still ached; a thick purple bruise ran from my eye to my chin. Orange hoops swung from her ears as she glanced away from my battered face.

My mother always hid her bruises. Cardigans on hot days, sunglasses, heavy make-up.

The woman glanced up again, asked, 'Single room?'

I lifted my hand to my bruised cheek – not to cover it, but to cool it. The woman's eyes followed my hand, then she was all bustle, leaping up from the wooden stool, searching for an unnecessary form, pressing a pen into my hand. In response to her contempt, I wanted to say: it was not a man who did this, but a boat. Not a punch but a storm. As though the shame from a punch would be mine. But instead I took my hand away, turned my cheek to her, let her have a good look while I said, 'Yes, I'll have a single room.' Her nails, covered in chipped black polish, tapped at the counter while I told her the number of the fleet account.

When she slid the key under the metal grille, I said, 'It's a bruise, not a birthmark.' I waited for her to say something else. To ask how, or why. But her orange hoops twirled furiously as she looked away, held up her hand to Karl. 'Yes, single room as well? On the fleet account?'

After the storm, in the dim early-morning light, we'd steamed half-heartedly back into Darwin docks for the shipwrights to spend two days fixing the boards. We were silent when we came alongside, silent when we stepped onto the dock, muted with the ache of disappointment, of unspoken failure. Still, two nights on solid ground, in a hotel paid for by the company, this was a promise of golden riches. The room was a small one, above the pub: a single bed, a tangerine chenille bedspread, a bedside lamp in the shape of the Statue of Liberty. Shared bathroom. Two days, though, without being woken every three hours; two days without having to speak to another person; two days of lying flat, reading and reading and reading. Two days of buying sweet-smelling cosmetics, hand creams, potions for my drying skin. I laid out the contents of the cotton bag I'd brought off the boat: three singlet tops, one skirt, a short polka-dotted dress, a pair of brown sandals, a plastic bag with toothbrush and cheap shampoo.

Though I turned the bag upside down, and shook it, and looked again, and shook again, I saw no wallet. I patted my body as though I were both cop and suspect, but there was no wallet, no means for buying books or potions or creams. Or, there was: but it was back on board the *Ocean Thief*, at the docks.

The pedestrian mall in the centre of Darwin had a broad tree in the centre, its leafy boughs spreading out across the path; with the ground still proving too unyielding, I stopped, leaned against the trunk, feeling the rough bark strange against my back. My head rested against the tree, my eyes closed for a moment.

'Kacey? Kacey?' A tap on the arm, a face grinning in front of me. A dark-haired, bikini-wearing girl. Long-limbed and from somewhere exotic, she was one of many faces at Lameroo Lodge. For three nights, or four, we'd shared a dorm room. She had snored lightly in her sleep, snuffling like a small animal. There, in front of the Darwin tree, her arms were held out as though for a hug, and I edged closer to the trunk. I couldn't recall her name, but I remembered that she spoke in exclamation points, her face beaming endlessly, the world always sunny, the slightest trace of a Swedish accent. 'How amazing! You're still here! I've got a job! In a café! The Golden Cup! Didn't you go on a boat?'

'A trawler. Yes.'

'That must be, um, exciting?'

My face was reflected in her sunglasses, round and distorted. I thought about the unwelcome memories that had begun swirling around me, courtesy of being stuck on a trawler. I said, 'It's hard.'

She stepped back, almost tripping, 'Oh my God, what happened to your face?'

I held my hand up, touched the place where I knew the bruising to be, said, 'It happened on the boat.'

'Someone did this to you? My God!'

'No. There was – a storm.'

'Oh.' The excitement slid slightly from her face.

I wanted the drama back, I wanted to shock her. I wanted to be the hero. 'We sank. The boat sank.'

'No!' Her face shone with interest.

'We couldn't get the nets up. During the storm. And the weight of the catch, the storm – I mean, it was insane.' I looked up to the matt sky. 'The boat went over, took water and went under.'

'My God! How did you – I mean, is everyone safe?'

'Pretty much. We managed to get the tender before we went under – so I had to wait in this tiny boat, just hoping for the best. It was pretty frightening.'

'Tender? Like love?'

'What? No. Like small boat. To get to shore. We managed to launch it and we waited the storm out. It was close, really close.'

'And you came to shore in this little boat?' She looked around, as though expecting the little boat to be tied to the sprawling tree.

'Another trawler picked us up.'

She shook her head so that her glossy hair shivered. 'What a shocking thing to happen.'

'Yes,' I said, 'it was, it was shocking. Truly.' And then I set off towards the duck pond, wobbling and weaving along the road, waiting for the ground to settle beneath me, or for my legs to settle on the road.

Now when I remember this I wonder if I knew all along, if I'd watched him, if I'd timed it. The *Ocean Thief* comes into view, smaller than I think of her, tattier, more battered. A black car is parked beside her, the boot open. Something makes me stop, hesitate, my heart thudding strangely. I can see a hand resting on the sill of the driver's window. I'm thinking: it's the shipwright, but so soon. Closer, I can see inside the boot: two battered freezer containers take up the whole boot space. A potato-shaped man snaps the lid on as I come close, then slams the boot shut. A figure emerges from the freezer room, wrapped in the thick red suit, his familiar moustache highlighting the pink patch of his face.

The hand on the windowsill of the car retracts, slams on to the car horn. The bright toot makes him turn to the car, makes him shout out something in French. The potato-shaped man – now I'm closer, I can see his wiry hair, his pitted skin – bolts to the passenger side of the car, slams the door. The tyres squeal as they reverse from the side of the dock.

Frenchie was peeling the freezer suit off as I climbed up to the deck, his face gleaming. 'My friends, they take my share of the catch.'

'Sure.' We were each entitled to a box or two of the catch to take home to family, to eat with friends, to do with what we wished. I watched him for a moment, both of us standing awkwardly, waiting for the other. I nodded towards the cabins. 'I forgot my wallet.'

Frenchie put his hand on my elbow. 'You remember you watch out for me? This is our deal.'

I shrugged. 'Sure.'

'This is my last season. I have had enough now. It's too much, this work. I need a good catch to leave here, to return to my life. To finish empty-handed, no, I cannot.' He wiped the damp from his face and said again, 'I look out for you, you look out for me. This is our deal. Without a good season, I have nothing.'

I thought: *What do you think any of us have? What do you think I have?* But I said nothing, just watched the bead of sweat in the hair of his moustache, watched it trickle to the top of his lip until he wiped it away, leaving a smear of dirt across his mouth, brown like chocolate, or mud.

I T TOOK THREE DAYS in the end for the boards to be repaired. On the last day before we headed back out to Bonaparte, I showered for twenty minutes, letting the hot water run over me. The water did not run cold, and it did not run to a trickle. Beneath my feet the tiles did not move, the soap had no layer of sludge, there was no build-up of grime, and it was simple, so simple, to be happy. I was scrubbed clean, the festering cuts on my hands and feet disinfected and dressed, my fingernails trimmed and clean, my clothes smelling only of laundry powder and the hotel dryer.

The sign above the Golden Cup extended into the mall, so it was easy to find. Inside, long, golden-hued wooden tables stretched the length of the café. I wondered if the golden wood was where the name came from, the name that made me think of Midas, or urine. The Swedish girl from Lameroo Lodge served me. Her hair was tied back in a perky ponytail, her teeth white and straight.

When she took my order, I said, 'My boat didn't sink. I'm sorry, that seemed more – God, I don't know, more exciting.' The air felt heavy, like it would swallow me. I added, 'I was hit in the face while I was trying to hold a torch on a boom. During a storm. It was – sorry. I don't know why I lied. I just thought it was a better story. It was someone else's story. It was stupid.'

'Yes. That is a very strange thing to do.' She peered at me. 'Your face looks a little better. A little.'

Frenchie was the last of us to get back to the docked *Ocean Thief*, a child's school backpack flung over one shoulder. He had a block of dark chocolate for me. When he handed it to me, Davey said, 'Why her and not me? I'd love some chocolate.'

Frenchie said, 'You've been near shops for three days. Buy your own. Kacey and me are taking care of each other.'

After the expanse of a two-star hotel room, my bunk seemed cramped. For the first time in months, I noticed the diesel smell, the public-toilet colour of the walls. There were no photos of family or friends in my bunk, nothing but the small collection of books which were my home. And my black lace-up shoes, tied to the end of the frame. Those shoes. Before I'd left to hitchhike along the highway, a woman had come to my mother's house, a fortune-teller. My mother paid her. It was, I suppose, my mother's way of giving me a blessing. 'Give me some jewellery,' she'd said. I had none. Not a ring, not a watch, nothing. I was bare. Just myself, my own skin. And that is how I thought I would always travel. I remember the woman with a head too small for her body, her henna-red hair spiralling down her back. Red lace was tied about her throat, and her lips were red too. She sat at my mother's pine table and I handed her what I had. One drawn-on brown eyebrow raised into a wrinkled forehead. At the time this seemed horrendous to me – the wrinkles, the chin, the eyebrow. Age seemed horrendous to me. The thought of it, the appearance of it. 'Give me anything,' she said. 'A ring, an earring, anything.'

I said, 'I haven't got anything.'

And then I gave her my shoe.

She said I would find love and I said that wasn't what I was looking for. She said I would find riches and I said, yes, sure, that's what I was looking for, why not? She didn't make me any other offers.

We were all quiet as we headed back out with the newly repaired boards, the freshly mended nets, the coiled and oiled ropes, the stock of fresh food. Bonaparte had not been good to us and there was little inclination to return. Still, Mick called us all up to the bow deck as the sun started to drop and we leaned against the gunwale, watching the sky turn gold and the water shine the colour back up to us. The door to the wheelhouse was open and we all heard the radio call, the broad Territory accent slicing the airwaves, the nasally voice. Steady and low, that voice asking all boats in the vicinity of the Tiwi Islands to be on the alert. *A crew member is missing.*

We crowded into the wheelhouse, leaning closer to the desk. *Deckhand. Missing since early oh-five-hundred-hours.*

The radio crackled and then the voice spoke again. *If the missing crew member is on board with you after pick-up, radio immediately. Repeat, immediately.*

The water unfurled ahead. The words of the radio sat heavy in the air. We didn't look at each other in the wheelhouse, didn't admit that we were waiting, hoping, for a second call, another voice crackling, *Got him, mate. Stupid dick toppled over, but we were right behind. Bringing him in now.* But there was no second voice, just the crackle and the thrum of the engine. Mick ran his hands along the desk, tapping against the glass of the radar. Slow beats patted my back in the place that I rested against the wheelhouse door, above the churning of the engine. Pat, thrum, pat, thrum. Davey was the one I thought about. If that missing boy were him –

But it could have been me, it could have been anyone. The season before, a cook had disappeared somewhere off Gove, barely three hours' coasting from the shabby town bowling club. Her name was Lucretia. She was a dancer. Had been, anyway, before the swansong of the Gulf and its easy money.

But this one was a boy. A deckhand younger than Davey, probably, with his gleaming grin and his excess of hair bouncing over his eyes. I could feel him with me in the wheelhouse, the missing boy. Could feel his breath, smell the fruity-salty smell of his skin. They didn't give his stats on the call-out, didn't give a description. What would we be looking for? A tall, lanky, brown-haired twenty-year-old? A blond, chubby seventeen-year-old growing his first beard? In the water, height is irrelevant. Still, I imagined him with tanned skin, green eyes, a sharp chin with a single dimple.

Daniel. They did say his name. His name was Daniel.

We steamed on, each of us imagining our own version of this boy, this Daniel, scanning the water side to side, knowing what we'd find, if we found anything at all.

FLECKS OF NAIL POLISH fall on to my beige dress. I've worried at my nails, chewing the corner of each in turn, tearing at the creamy polish. Hoping, perhaps, to unpeel the whole sheet of it, and then to unpeel my own skin, my innards, my whole self. Walking up the three steps to the witness box, my sensible low heels make a dull click. Someone at the back of the courtroom coughs repeatedly as though a fur ball is stuck in their throat and my hand goes to my own throat in sympathy.

It begins gently enough. The public prosecutor asks me my name, where I live. He asks me if I got a taxi on the night in question.

'Yes,' I say, 'I got a taxi home from a party.'

'Can you remember the man who drove the taxi?'

'Yes.'

'Can you point to that man?'

'Yes,' I say, and I point, but I cannot look at him.

You see, even in this way, I am a bad girl, a bad witness. Why could I not look at him? Was I ashamed? Of my own behaviour? People who are lying often avoid eye contact. People who are frightened do, too. People who are distressed, they avoid eye contact. People who are so stuck, so lost, that they don't know how to raise their eyes.

After the prosecutor walks me through the events of the Night In Question, the man's barrister steps up, adjusting his tie. He smiles at me, then looks at the paper in his hand. 'You fell asleep in the taxi for twenty minutes, yes?'

'Yes,' I say. 'I think so. I'm not sure.'

'Not sure?'

'No, because I—'

'Because you'd consumed rather a lot of alcohol that night, hadn't you?' And then his mouth twists and he holds up a plastic bag. 'Are these your underpants from that night?'

Inside the plastic my pearl-coloured French knickers have been pegged into shape so that you can see the line of them, the way they gleam, the silk inviting touch, the way the pant leg flares open like shorts.

'Did you,' the barrister asks, 'have underpants on under these shorts?'

I say, 'I'm sorry?'

'Underpants.'

'They are my underpants. They are – ' and here I begin crying ' – they're French knickers. It's a – women used to—'

He says, 'I know what they are and what their history is.' He nods to the jury. One woman shakes her head slightly as she looks at the plastic bag. Brown hair curls neatly around her chin, her hands clasped together on the bench.

Although it doesn't matter, not now, I add, 'My friend gave them to me. My girlfriend.'

'Girlfriend?'

I am crying properly now.

'And won't it help your case,' he says, 'if you are distressed?'

The judge inclines his head, his whole body following. I remember him with glasses, horn-rimmed, and with excess flesh wobbling slightly on his cheeks. To the court transcriber he says, 'Note that the witness *is* distressed.' To the barrister, he says, 'That line is unacceptable.'

I cannot say thank you, though I want to.

The barrister begins again. 'You were so very drunk, weren't you, that you left these *loose shorts* in the taxi, is that right? Though, in fact, they barely needed removing.' He holds the plastic bag up again, highlighting the wide-open leg, the lack of elastication.

Again, the judge leans forward, the light bouncing off his glasses, and the barrister is chastised.

'Why is it,' the barrister says, 'that you told the police officers "I *think* I have been raped"?'

'I wasn't sure. I didn't know if he – if it was his finger inside me or—'

'You weren't *sure*? You couldn't tell the *difference*?'

'It was dark. I wanted to be careful with the truth. And I had been drinking.'

'Yes, you had. Quite a lot by the look of this list. One bottle of cider, two bottles of wine, two glasses of strong liquor.' He smiles at the jury. 'I think I would be *quite* forgetful if I drank that much alcohol.'

'I didn't have all that alone. I shared it with my friend.'

The curly-haired woman on the jury compresses her lips, looks sideways at the woman beside her. Again, that slight shake of the head.

The barrister runs his fingers along his collar, tugging at it as though letting air into his chest. His hair has a shine to it; his skin is unblemished. He is, I think, the kind of man I might have fantasised about marrying, if I were a different kind of girl. The kind of man who might have saved me. But he is not here to save me. He is here to destroy me.

He asks me if I have a boyfriend (I don't), if I have sex often (I do), and what I hope to gain by dragging this poor man to court. He points out that I have been to drama school, that I dropped out of university. He asks me four times how many people were at the party, and each time my answer is different.

He says, 'Do you find it hard to keep track of your stories?'

My face grows hot and the polyester of the dress starts to itch. I scratch at my neck, and then at my face. When I look in the mirror later, I have scratch marks on my neck, long tracks that match the red blotches on my cheeks.

I can't remember how long it lasts. It seems like hours, days. He paces up and down, and I scratch at my neck. The jury look at me, and then at the man's pretty wife. Eventually, as though summing up my school report, the barrister says, 'In your statement, which I have here, you are unable to be certain whether you are speaking of a finger or of another body part. That is how intoxicated you were. I put it to you that in this state of extreme inebriation you invited *this poor man* to have sexual intercourse with you and then you regretted it. Isn't that right?'

Now, when I look back at myself, trembling, my arms folded across my chest, looking for just one kind face in that courtroom, I want to applaud. Because I am resourceless, it's true. But, somehow, the fury in me will not be daunted. Pressing against the ledge, I say, 'Whatever the body part—whether it was a penis, a finger or a feather—I did not invite it. I did not ask for anything to be put into my vagina by that man.'

Eyebrows raised, he turns away.

But my one little outburst is not enough. After three days, the jury find him not guilty and, by extension, they find me guilty.

For three days I have held my arms across my chest, have kept my lips closed. For three days I have contained myself, held up by my own string and by that tiny angry worm flicking and turning deep in my gut. But now, my string is cut, the worm is sliced, and I sit outside the courtroom wailing and wailing and wailing so loudly and for so long that I have to be escorted from the building. When I stop crying, I feel like there is nothing left of me, no tears, no marrow, no bone.

We know the figures – I know the figures. How unlikely it is to get a conviction in a sexual assault trial. We know – I know – that it is not me on trial. *And yet, and yet, and yet*: always, in these stories, the victory, the fist-pumping celebration, the moment the girl is vindicated – that moment is always the one in which the man is found guilty.

So: if he is not guilty? What then? What am I?

Did I have to be an innocent to be innocent?

I SENT OFF THE FORMS to see the transcripts and the police records. What did they write about me, I wondered, this drunken girl with windmill arms and dripping make-up? First, I called the Office of Public Prosecutions.

The woman asked, 'Are you the victim in the case?' Her voice dropped a notch when she said the word *victim*. I imagined her leaning into the mouthpiece, bobbing her head, forming her mouth into a sympathetic circle.

'Yes,' I said. I had no wish to offer the alternate word, *survivor*. It's obvious I survived. And, anyway, survivor would reframe the story so that the impact of the assault was entirely to do with me. Survivor means I've done well, been a good girl. Victim means that I have failed. These words remove the perpetrator and make the assault about me. They're both wrong, but I had no other word, so I said, 'Yes, I am the victim.' The woman mumbled and rustled some papers, put me on hold for a while, asked me to call back the following day. I did, hoping that the transcript would exist, hoping that it wouldn't.

That night, I called my most longstanding friend, in Oxford. I've known her since I was twenty-one, the year after all this happened, the year after I was changed. When I met her my muscle was already being built; I'd leaped into the open sea from the top of a fishing trawler, I'd spent nights and days winching up nets, clambering along decks and booms, months responding only to my body and to the work of the sea; I'd sifted through the mud and murk of memory, had been undone and had begun to put myself back together. She has only known me as the person I became.

She flickered into view on the screen, a sunny Oxford garden flowering behind her, a single apple tree budding into life. While she brushed her hair for the day ahead, and I prepared mine for the night, I told her about the call to the Office of Public Prosecutions, the way the woman's voice had lowered. My friend nodded sympathetically, tugging at her hair. Then her expression changed – I could see the moment that she'd registered – and she swivelled back to the camera. 'Wait,' she said. 'You never – I never knew this. About the taxi driver? About – oh my God, I'm so sorry. And he got off? Jesus.'

'I guess there wasn't enough evidence. From my memory, there really wasn't any evidence that he'd even touched me. I mean, what was a jury to do?' I had taken into myself the slick swirl of their story, the sorry questions, the churning doubts.

She was still shaking her head, hands to her cheeks. 'I'm so, so sorry, darling.'

And that is why I never told her. Why I shook the dust from my feet and left it behind me, along with those transcripts. I didn't want pity, couldn't bear it, didn't want to be known as a victim or as a survivor. Not of that, not of the court case, not of poverty, not of the broken bits of family, the cracked shards that I had glued together to make a whole. When I unfolded that map and ran my finger along the edge of the largest island on earth, I wanted to set fire to those questions. And when I spent those nights being tossed about in that sea, I wanted to undo what had been done to me.

Some months after sending off my request for the records, I received an email responding to my query. Attached to the email, a series of police statements. I opened the attachments and then closed my computer again quickly, as though it contained a virus. For several days I avoided looking at it; nausea twisted in my gut when I thought of it, when I thought of facing her, of seeing her anew, the girl that I was.

After a week, I opened the documents, my hands shaky. My statement was there, also the statement from the taxi driver who assaulted me and one from the driver who picked me up. There was also a statement from the biologist who found the perpetrator's semen on my stomach and in my vaginal canal. And one from the detective who went to the driver's house the next day, who drove with him to the rubbish bin on a public street where he had thrown my silk underpants and my wallet. My head felt cloudy, as though I were deep underwater.

Certain phrases had been underlined, but only in my statement: *I fell asleep again, I don't know for how long; when I woke up the car was stationary, and the taxi driver was kneeling over me; I could tell I was not wearing my underpants. I do not know where they were. I was wearing them when I got inside the taxi; perhaps I was asleep for twenty minutes, I am not sure.* I can't make sense of the underlining, what the common thread is. Early in the statement, underlined, there is a snatch of dialogue:

He said, 'Can I take you for coffee?' I said no. He said, 'Can I take you out dancing?' Again I said no. He asked me two or three more times if he could take me for coffee and each time my answer was the same.

The detective, in his statement, describes driving with another detective and the owner of the cab company to the man's apartment. They walk up the stairs. Concrete, I think, these stairs would be, in keeping with the style of apartment blocks built in the 1970s. The detective knocks on the door and, after a moment, the door opens. A bearded man stands in front of him, the apartment behind him is in shadow. The bearded man says: *I know why you're here, fellas. It's about the girl.*

BONAPARTE DIDN'T CHANGE during the days we were docked, didn't suddenly start giving up prawns, calming its storms. Wind churned and churled again, and still each catch was thin. We folded cartons between catches, counting them off glumly. For five days we dropped the nets in and hauled them out and sorted and batched and put on the thick ski clothes for the freezer room and took turns climbing down, piling the boxed prawns to the front, counting them off again, noting that there were still not enough. On the fifth day it was my turn to be swaddled in the thick freezer suit and to climb down to the swirling cold air.

After the expanding heat of the deck, there was something soothing in the freezer room, the white of it, the cold. Davey waddled around while I lifted myself up to the shelf, pushing the stock to the back. I shouldered my way to the packs at the back of the tray, only half listening to Davey babbling like a child. There were rows of boxes – our entire catch, our entire income, parcelled up, ready to be cashed in for all our escape tickets. A wedding ring for Mick, a rental bond for Davey, a skippering course for Karl, a ticket out for me – a place to finally begin my proper story. Those packages meant all of that to us. It wasn't the first time that I'd counted them out in my head, like a rosary, soothing myself with the calculation of what each batch would be worth. There was never enough, but there was something. This time, I could hear Davey's voice – he was telling me a lengthy story, something about the factory he'd worked in, a fire or a fire alarm, the way his mum, who was a total legend, had gone round there and dragged him out – but as I bumped against the cartons, I could feel the difference in the weight of them. Squatting down, I shoved some of them forward; I could hear the thud of the frozen catch, feel the weight. Perhaps three rows were packed full. But behind them, row upon row of boxes that did not rattle when I moved them, that contained only the weight of air. Row upon row of empty boxes, folded and stacked to look like they were full.

I stayed on my knees on the tray while the sharp air cut into me. Those boxes were all our work, all our sleeplessness, all our storms, all our bruises, all our hopes. Davey's voice was muffled, but I could hear him anyway, calling, 'Kacey? You okay? Are we done? I hate it in here. I'm going up.'

Then the dull clang of his feet on the ladder, the creak and clack of the hatch lifting and closing.

I stayed there for a while, counting off the empty cartons, letting the hope seep out of me slowly, and then I went to find him.

The engine room was dark, suffocatingly loud. I don't know how he stood it, with his earphones and his shirtless body and the steam on his moustache. I tapped him on the arm, mouthed, You bastard. He shook his head and shrugged elaborately. I shoved him in the chest and pointed to the ladder, waited for him to follow me up. At the stern I scraped at the gunwale with a palette knife, keeping my eyes down, and when I felt him beside me, I didn't look up but said, 'You stole the catch.'

He leaned on the gunwale, back to the water, eyes to the wheelhouse. 'You already knew this.'

'I bloody didn't, Frenchie. The whole catch.'

'Not all.'

'Most.'

He took a pack of tobacco from his back pocket, his yellowed finger trembling slightly as he rolled a thin cigarette. 'I am an old man and I cannot keep doing this. The catch is too small for all of us to share. And it is time for me to stop. To retire. So.' He took a drag; when he pulled the rollie away, a shred of tobacco clung to his lip.

I was looking at him now. 'We all need it.'

'But there is not enough to share.'

'Christ, Frenchie. There isn't now. You've screwed us all over.'

'No. No, I was being screwed over myself. You need to understand – I needed this. All my life I have—'

'We've all worked. Why should you have it?'

'I need it most. You are all young and pretty. And you're a girl. You don't need this. You will be fine.' He spat the tobacco away, then looked down at me. 'And you cover my back. This is our deal, Kacey.'

In the galley, Mick was standing at the bench, arms folded, staring at the floor, Davey and Karl standing opposite. Coffee grains were scattered on the bench, bleeding brown blobs into the laminate. I knew before I asked, but I asked anyway. 'What's up? What's happened?'

Mick kept staring at the floor. 'They found the boy. The decky.'

Karl rubbed at the coffee grains, flicking the brown spots to the sink, scratching and scratching. 'He was tied to a gas canister.'

Davey added, 'Like a barrel. A weight. But he floated.'

I waited for more, but they were silent. 'But he's…?'

'No. There'll be an inquest in Darwin.' Mick's voice wavered. 'They'll probably rule suicide.'

We stayed like that for a while, standing in the galley, staring at the dirty green floor, each of us thinking about the deckhand floating alone in the Timor Sea, thinking about what might have led to that moment, and what might follow.

The engine cut out and there was silence, and then without thinking about it, I said, 'Frenchie stole most of the catch. He's replaced the boxes in the freezer room with empty ones. This whole season has been worthless. We've got nothing.'

Except, I thought, I do have something. I have this, only this: I am here, alive, on the *Ocean Thief*, and not floating, tied to a barrel, skin seeping away into the salt.

By the time we motored back to Darwin, the storms had started to calm, the water was smooth and settled, the sun blasting down again. Frenchie took the mattress from his bunk down to the engine room and refused to leave, refused to speak, refused to cook.

We kept under power and ate toast and cheese and packets of biscuits and we sat silently at the galley table. What was to be said? We had failed, that was all. Each of us used the time returning to shore to count off our own disappointments, to find our own way back.

The flat shape of the land started to come into view, a cloudy haze huddling over it. Only the plain black terns and the gulls stayed on the booms as we came in from the heads, the wind playing with their feathers. On the upper deck, I pressed my back against the heat of the wheelhouse wall and tried to sketch them in the end pages of one of my journals.

There was a ribbon in the journal I'd carried with me from my bunk, and the page it fell open at had a list of names. Some of the names were scribbled in capital letters, some in tiny pen. Some names had clearly been written in the dark, after one of the feverish dreams and surging memories that accompanied me in those months on the *Ocean Thief*. Some were underlined, others circled on the outer margins of the page.

The list was long. My father was on it, and Ben Billman, David Fox with his louche grin and uninvited fucking. Some of them were names: Tony de Ropp with his father's car; the boy who lived next door to me with his soft boy's penis; the bass player with his unwanted sperm; the high school science teacher who stood below the stairs and watched me walk up them, barely even hiding his gaze; the boys at school who, daily, asked me to sit on their faces. Some were titles without names: the boy on his bicycle giving me a linguistics lesson; the man wanking on the end of the phone; the man on the sailing boat with his wrinkled testicles sticking out of his shorts; the man on the street doing the same; the taxi driver; his barrister. Two pages of them circled and underlined, boxes and arrows drawn around them and through them. Around some of them, I'd doodled sharp spikes, or barbed wire, like a prison fence.

A corridor of breeze lifted as we came closer to shore. I could make out the outlines of the docks, the boats and buildings, and I didn't want to step back onto land carrying that list. I'd carried it so far and for so long; I was done with it. I wanted to be done with it.

The pages made a pleasing shred as I ripped them from the journal. It was bound with string, and I had to tug to get the second page to come away. I tore it first lengthways, into narrow strips, and then I tore the strips into gum-sized pieces. Fumes mixed with the smell of salt and I closed my eyes, inhaled, tried to commit it to memory.

I stood on the port side, away from the shadow of the land. I could see the land on one side, and on the other the long stretch of the horizon. Light slanted across the water and it was lit up so brightly that I saw everything – the horizon, the harbour, the whole world – with a shining halo. When the wind rose, I lifted my hands and opened my fists. Paper pieces scattered on the breeze, swirling in the air like snow, or breadcrumbs.

Gulls lifted from the boom, squawking and swooping, fighting over the flimsy pieces of paper sifting on the wind. Some pieces drifted to the surface of the water, where gulls fought over them. Although no one could hear me, I shouted, 'It's not bread, you fools.' I remembered, then, a quotation written on the blackboard during my stint in a Catholic girls' school, a quotation from the Book of Job. *Tears have been my food, day and night.*

This list was not food.

Those men were not my story.

We came into the shelter of the bay and I went into the dark cabin for the last time, dragging my backpack out into the galley. I stripped the bed, folded my spotted cloth and put it in the top of my pack, and I peeled my sketch of Robbie from the wall. Damp had seeped into the paper, making it mottled and brittle. I threw it into the galley bin.

I could hear shouting from the dock, the slowing of the engine; we juddered as the hull hit the side of the wall. My pack felt lighter on my back when I lifted it; I was stronger now. Karl and Davey were waiting for me on the deck; Karl in his board shorts, chest bare, unchanged from the months on board, and Davey, tanned now, and without the soft milky curves on his face. Three cops were waiting on the concrete dock. Frenchie went without a word, without a glance. He threw his bag over the hull, and one of the cops caught it for him. Frenchie was loud and blustery, shouting down, 'Good catch, mate.'

The cop called back, 'You're the catch, buddy.'

Frenchie laughed. They had nothing on him.

We stayed on deck, watching the blue police light flashing; Frenchie ducking his head as he slid into the back of the car, lifting his hand in a middle-finger salute. There he was, the hero of his own story: unwashed and red-eyed in the back of an overheated Territory police car. Karl hugged me, for the first time, and then he leaped down to the dock. Davey shook my hand, all formal. I have no idea where either of them went, what they became. There are men like them everywhere in the Territory, men like them on boats or in the middle of nowhere. Middle-aged now, rough-faced and thick-set. Some of them are pickled with booze. Some are kind, some are not. But I want to remember those boys as they were: soft-skinned, not yet turned.

In my snug cabin I had left a pile of books – *On the Road, The Catcher in the Rye, The Glass Bead Game, Steppenwolf,* all the boys' own adventures – tottering on the side of the bunk, waiting to be thrown out or passed on, to be read by someone bored or lonely or desperate or drowning. It didn't matter. I didn't want them any more.

I'd seen the beautiful horizon, and I'd seen bilge and blood dripping into the sea. I'd slept with crocodiles and I'd swum with sharks. This girl's story, my own story, was all I had, all I needed. The truth: imperfect, reeking of failure and of the need to begin again. But it was my own. I made it.

WHEN I THINK BACK on it, time flutters like the image of the sea on a heat-filled day, the haze floating over it, the shapes shimmering in the light, coming only slowly into focus. Salt in the air, the tangle of ropes, the jangle of boat stays. There I am, hanging by one arm from the trawling boom, ready to drop to the deep and desperate blue. Below me, the deep aqua field, the swirling of fins.

There was only one photo from that time: I was round-faced, with a scarf tied about my head, and squinted at the camera, sun blaring into my eyes. In the corner of the frame, a coil of rope. I found it years later, in the drawer of my mother's pine dresser. I'd flown out from Oxford, my skin prickling with rage, bubbling into red rashes the way it always did on those return visits to that town whose name I do not care to remember. We'd raked through her cupboards, excavating photos, old school reports, and then we threw the dresser out too. It was battered by then, marked with years of grime, the top of it scratched so deeply you couldn't see the original pine. We left it on the verge along with a load of my mother's possessions, the culmination of a life, piled on to a pyre that reached beyond her low bungalow windows.

The council truck came to collect it all and the man driving was so skinny his skin bagged around his shoulders. He wore a marked white singlet and the skin slapped in folds around the fabric. I couldn't look away though it made me want to gag, the sight of it flapping like a sail on a slow day. 'Take it all,' I said. 'Burn it if you want. Nothing here has value.' I threw the photo on the pile too. I didn't want it, didn't understand yet what it meant.

I'd brought a friend, Simon. For moral support or something. He waited in the car, his eyes straight ahead, though I know he was horrified. Naturally I'd talked about this, what I came from, how I formed myself, what it took. But no one thought I meant *this* – not this squat bungalow, the peeling paint, the wilting pile of broken furniture and lost plastic items.

When I got in the car, he didn't say a word. We sat in silence for a while, then I said, 'Okay. Let's go.'

When we turned on to the main road, he said, 'Did you grow up there?'

'No,' I said. 'I didn't. Not really. I grew up on the *Ocean Thief*.' For effect, I added: 'I grew up in the middle of the Timor Sea.'

He turned his head, then, and I had to tap him on the shoulder, just playfully. 'Eyes on the road, Simon, hands on the wheel.'

The Timor Sea. Carpentaria. Bloody Bonaparte. I thought they'd be the end of me. But they were my beginning.

Acknowledgements

In the years since I stepped off the *Ocean Thief*, fishing in the gulf has become more regulated and controlled. The beleaguered fleet I worked on was split up and sold on; the remodelled *Ocean Thief* eventually finding its home as part of Austral Fisheries. I am immensely grateful to David Carter and all at Austral Fisheries for allowing me the opportunity to spend time on the boat as it is now. Thanks also go to the hard-working and hilarious crew of the present-day *Ocean Thief*, who took time out of their season to detour and collect me, made space for me on the boat and were incredibly generous and patient. Thanks are due, too, to ArtsNSW for providing the support for that trip.

I am always grateful to the Copyright Agency for the work they do in support of authors and their intellectual property. I am particularly thankful for the generous award of the Author Fellowship, which allowed me to give proper attention to this book. Additional thanks to Terri Janke and Company, in particular to Ruby Langton-Batty.

I am thankful, as ever, to my steadfast agent Catherine Drayton, publisher Jane Palfreyman and editor Ali Lavau, as well as Christa Munns and the whole brilliant bunch at Allen & Unwin.

Extra thanks to Christine Madill for her enthusiasm and generosity via #AuthorsForFireys.

My thanks also to each of the magnificent writers who make the Australian Writers Mentoring Program such a joy: Carrie

Tiffany, Toni Jordan, Margo Lanagan, James Bradley, Mark Tredinnick, Jacqueline Kent, Alison Croggon, Ross Grayson Bell, Malcolm Knox, Nick Earls, Ashley Hay, Stephanie Dowrick and Jaclyn Moriarty. And also to Jill Dawson, my dear ally.

I will forever owe a debt of gratitude to Victoria, the first person to demonstrate to me that it might be possible to live a creative life.

Most importantly, my endless thanks to Richard Griffiths – first and finest reader, sharpest eye, keenest ear, most trusted human. I will always be grateful.

Finally, thanks go to my children – Seren, whose wisdom and courage inspire me daily, and Tali, whose curiosity, calm and kindness give me hope.

Author's note

The line 'I felt the wet push its black thumb-balls in, the night you died' on page 176 is from Kenneth Slessor's masterpiece, 'Five Bells' (*Selected Poems*, 2014). Extracted with permission of HarperCollins Australia.

The Philip Larkin poem I refer to on page 135 is 'The Importance of Elsewhere'. It can be found in *The Complete Poems*, published by Faber & Faber in 2012.

About the author

KATHRYN HEYMAN is a novelist, essayist and scriptwriter. Her sixth novel, *Storm and Grace*, was published to critical acclaim in 2017. Her first novel, *The Breaking*, was shortlisted for the Stakis Prize for the Scottish Writer of the Year and longlisted for the Orange Prize. Other awards include an Arts Council of England Writers Award, the Wingate Scholarship, the Southern Arts Award, and nominations for the Edinburgh Fringe Critics' Awards, the Kibble Prize, and the West Australian Premier's Book Awards, as well as the Copyright Agency Author Fellowship for *Fury*.

Kathryn Heyman's several plays for BBC radio include *Far Country* and *Moonlite's Boy*, inspired by the life of bushranger Captain Moonlite. Two of her novels have been adapted for BBC radio: *Keep Your Hands on the Wheel* as a play and *Captain Starlight's Apprentice* as a five-part dramatic serial.

Heyman has held several writing fellowships, including the Scottish Arts Council Writing Fellowship at the University of Glasgow, and a Royal Literary Fund Writing Fellowship at Westminster College, Oxford. She taught creative writing for the University of Oxford and is now Conjoint Professor in Humanities at the University of Newcastle. In 2012, she founded the Australian Writers Mentoring Program.

www.kathrynheyman.com
www.writermentors.com